CW01669551

THE ESSENTIAL MICROSOFT SHAREPOINT 2025 GUIDE FOR BEGINNERS

LOUGANA NARRUSE

INTRODUCTION

In an era where seamless communication, collaboration, and information accessibility are vital to business success, navigating tools that facilitate these elements becomes crucial. SharePoint stands at the forefront of such tools, offering not just a platform but a robust ecosystem designed to enhance teamwork, streamline processes, and centralize knowledge. For beginners stepping into the vast landscape of SharePoint, this journey can be both exciting and daunting. However, with the right guidance and foundational understanding, anyone can harness the full potential of this powerful tool.

SharePoint has evolved significantly since its inception, transforming from a basic document-sharing portal into a highly customizable, multifaceted platform that serves organizations of all sizes. Microsoft has invested continually in enhancing SharePoint's usability, security, and adaptability, making it an indispensable asset in today's dynamic digital workplaces. This guide is crafted with the goal of helping beginners develop a strong footing, providing essential knowledge that will enable them to navigate SharePoint with confidence and agility.

One of SharePoint's defining characteristics is its versatility. While at its core, SharePoint functions as a tool for document management and team collaboration, its applications stretch far beyond these capabilities. Today, it can be configured to serve as an intranet, a file repository, a content management system, and even a platform for building business applications. For someone new to SharePoint, this flexibility can be overwhelming. Understanding the fundamental features is key to leveraging its potential effectively.

This guide begins with a thorough introduction to SharePoint, covering its primary components, functions, and the different versions available. A solid grasp of the basics sets the stage for users to appreciate SharePoint's broader applications. Through the initial chapters, beginners will gain insights into the layout, tools, and functionalities that make up the SharePoint environment. This foundational knowledge is invaluable, as it enables new users to recognize and utilize key features more effectively.

For individuals stepping into the SharePoint platform for the first time, the user interface and home page layout are critical first impressions. SharePoint's home page serves as the central hub from which users can access various components, navigate libraries, lists, and sites, and manage their workspaces. This guide provides a straightforward walkthrough of the home page, helping beginners understand how to locate and interact with essential elements. The home page is designed to streamline access to shared content, making it a cornerstone of SharePoint's usability.

Accessibility is one of SharePoint's significant strengths. Not only can users access it through web browsers on desktops, but it also provides compatibility with mobile devices. SharePoint's mobile access and responsive design ensure that users can stay connected to their team and resources regardless of location. For the modern workforce, this flexibility is invaluable. This guide will delve into mobile access capabilities, exploring ways to use SharePoint on tablets, smartphones, and other devices. By understanding mobile access, beginners can make the most of SharePoint's offerings even when on the go.

Libraries and lists are central to SharePoint's functionality. They enable users to store, organize, and manage data in various formats, making it easy for teams to collaborate on documents, track project milestones, and manage information. Mastering libraries and lists is essential for beginners, as these components are frequently used in day-to-day activities. This guide will walk readers through the setup and use of libraries and lists, offering practical tips for organizing and accessing data efficiently. By the end of this section, beginners will understand how to create, modify, and manage libraries and lists to suit their unique requirements.

SharePoint's collaborative features are among its most impactful aspects. In a digital landscape where teamwork is crucial to success, SharePoint offers tools specifically designed to facilitate collaboration. From document co-authoring to task management, SharePoint enables teams to work together seamlessly, even if they are in different locations. This guide explores various collaboration tools within SharePoint, offering insights into how these tools can improve productivity and ensure that team members stay connected and aligned on projects.

Managing access and permissions is another critical skill for anyone working with SharePoint. Ensuring that the right people have access to the right resources is fundamental to maintaining security and efficiency. SharePoint provides a detailed permissions framework that allows for customization of access at various levels. For beginners, understanding permissions can be challenging, but it is an essential skill to master. This guide breaks down the permissions structure in an accessible way, helping users understand how to grant, modify, and manage access based on role requirements.

Customization is a vital aspect of SharePoint that enables organizations to tailor the platform to their specific needs. Whether it's modifying the layout, adjusting the navigation, or integrating third-party applications, SharePoint's customization capabilities are vast. This guide introduces beginners to the concept of customization, highlighting how they can personalize their SharePoint experience without overwhelming complexity. By understanding customization options, beginners can transform their SharePoint environment to reflect their organization's unique workflows and branding.

Advanced users often rely on SharePoint's document libraries for more than just storing files. These libraries come equipped with version control, metadata management, and check-in/check-out features that ensure documents are accessible, organized, and secure. For beginners, working with document libraries may initially seem daunting, but this guide provides a step-by-step approach to managing documents effectively. Understanding document libraries will enable users to maintain organization and control over files, an essential skill for any SharePoint user.

One of SharePoint's standout features is its advanced search functionality. As data accumulates, finding specific documents or pieces of information can become challenging. SharePoint's search capabilities are robust, allowing users to locate content based on various criteria quickly. This guide introduces beginners to search tools and techniques that can enhance content discovery, saving time and improving efficiency.

In today's digital landscape, security and privacy are paramount concerns. SharePoint's security features are designed to protect sensitive information and ensure that data remains accessible only to authorized individuals. This guide addresses SharePoint's security mechanisms, helping beginners understand how to keep their environment secure. By exploring best practices for permissions, encryption, and compliance, beginners can make informed decisions about managing data securely within SharePoint.

The importance of disaster recovery and backup cannot be overstated in the digital age. Organizations rely heavily on digital infrastructure, making data loss a significant risk. SharePoint includes disaster recovery and backup options to mitigate this risk. This guide concludes by discussing strategies for implementing effective disaster recovery and backup plans, ensuring that data is protected and recoverable in the event of a system failure.

In summary, this guide is crafted to support beginners in their SharePoint journey, providing a structured path from foundational knowledge to advanced functionalities. SharePoint, with all its depth and capabilities, can significantly enhance collaboration, productivity, and information management for any organization. Through this guide, users will acquire the skills and understanding needed to make the most of SharePoint's features and customize it to their specific needs.

The journey into SharePoint may appear complex, but with the right insights and guidance, even beginners can navigate it with confidence and efficiency. This guide aims to empower users with practical knowledge and hands-on skills, enabling them to transform SharePoint from a seemingly complex tool into a valuable asset for their work and team.

CONTENTS

INTRODUCTION iii
CONTENTS ix

Chapter 1: Introducing to SharePoint 1
Chapter 2: Keyboard shortcuts in SharePoint 25
Chapter 3: Navigating the SharePoint Home Page 31
Chapter 4: Accessing SharePoint - Web and Desktop 39
Chapter 5: Mobile Access and Responsive Design 42
Chapter 6: Mastering Libraries and Lists 51
Chapter 7: Managing SharePoint Access 60
Chapter 8: Effective Collaboration Tools 64
Chapter 9: Records Management and Archiving 79
Chapter 10: Customizing Your SharePoint Site 83
Chapter 11: Working with Document Libraries 87
Chapter 12: Advanced Search and Content Discovery 93
Chapter 13: Managing Permissions 100
Chapter 14: Ensuring SharePoint Security 106
Chapter 15: Disaster Recovery and Backup Strategies 112

CONCLUSION 119

CHAPTER 1: INTRODUCING TO SHAREPOINT

1.1 WHAT IS SHAREPOINT?

Microsoft SharePoint is a robust platform designed to facilitate collaboration, document management, and content sharing within organizations. Initially launched in 2001, SharePoint has evolved into a comprehensive suite of tools that integrates seamlessly with other Microsoft products like Office 365, Microsoft Teams, and OneDrive, making it a central hub for workplace productivity.

At its core, SharePoint is a web-based platform that enables businesses to create websites. These websites can be used to store, organize, share, and access information from any device, ensuring that employees can collaborate efficiently regardless of their location. SharePoint's versatility allows it to be tailored to various business needs, from simple document storage solutions to complex workflows and business intelligence systems.

One of SharePoint's primary functions is its ability to manage documents. Organizations can store vast amounts of files in SharePoint document libraries, which provide version control, metadata management, and advanced search capabilities. This makes it easy to track changes, find specific documents quickly, and ensure that employees are always working with the most up-to-date information. Additionally, SharePoint integrates with Microsoft Office, allowing users to edit documents directly within the platform without the need to download them first.

SharePoint also excels in collaboration. Teams can create dedicated sites, known as team sites, where they can share documents, calendars, tasks, and other resources. These team sites can be customized with various web parts, such as news feeds, document libraries, and discussion boards, to suit the specific needs of the team. This centralized approach to information sharing helps to break down silos within organizations, fostering better communication and collaboration.

Another key feature of SharePoint is its workflow automation capabilities. Businesses can automate routine tasks, such as document approval processes, using SharePoint's built-in workflow tools or Microsoft Power Automate, which integrates seamlessly with SharePoint. This not only saves time but also reduces the risk of human error, ensuring that processes are followed consistently and accurately.

SharePoint is also highly customizable. Organizations can create their own site designs and templates, tailor the user interface to match their branding, and develop custom applications using SharePoint Framework (SPFx). This flexibility allows businesses to create solutions that precisely meet their needs, whether it's a simple intranet site or a complex enterprise content management system.

Security is another area where SharePoint shines. It offers granular permissions settings, allowing administrators to control who has access to what information. This ensures that sensitive data is protected and only accessible to those who need it. SharePoint also supports compliance with various regulatory standards, making it a suitable choice for industries with strict data governance requirements.

In addition to its core features, SharePoint integrates with a wide range of third-party applications and services. This extensibility allows organizations to leverage existing investments in other technologies and create a cohesive digital workplace. For example, SharePoint can be integrated with customer relationship management (CRM) systems, enterprise resource planning (ERP) systems, and other line-of-business applications, providing a unified platform for managing business processes.

The modern SharePoint experience, introduced in SharePoint Online and SharePoint 2019, offers a more intuitive and responsive user interface compared to its predecessors. This modern experience includes improved page layouts, easier navigation, and enhanced mobile compatibility, making it easier for users to interact with SharePoint sites on any device.

In conclusion, Microsoft SharePoint is a powerful platform that supports document management, collaboration, workflow automation, and customization. Its integration with other Microsoft products and third-party services, along with its robust security features, makes it an essential tool for businesses looking to improve productivity and streamline operations. Whether you're a small business or a large enterprise, SharePoint offers the flexibility and scalability to meet your organization's needs, both now and in the future.

1.2 THE DEVELOPMENT HISTORY OF SHAREPOINT

The development history of Microsoft SharePoint is a fascinating journey that spans over two decades, highlighting the platform's evolution from a basic document management tool to a comprehensive solution for enterprise collaboration, content management, and process automation.

The Early Years (2001-2006)

SharePoint's story begins in 2001 with the launch of SharePoint Portal Server 2001 and SharePoint Team Services. These early versions were designed to address the growing need for document management and team collaboration tools. SharePoint Portal Server offered document storage, search capabilities, and basic content management, while SharePoint Team Services provided team sites for collaboration. Although rudimentary by today's standards, these initial offerings laid the groundwork for SharePoint's future development.

MOSS 2007 and WSS 3.0: A Significant Leap

In 2006, Microsoft released Office SharePoint Server 2007 (MOSS 2007) and Windows SharePoint Services 3.0 (WSS 3.0). This release marked a significant leap forward in terms of functionality and usability. MOSS 2007 introduced new features such as content management, business intelligence, and improved search capabilities. It also integrated more deeply with Microsoft Office, making it easier for users to collaborate on documents and projects. WSS 3.0, the free version, provided basic collaboration tools and served as the foundation for MOSS 2007.

The 2007 release was pivotal because it positioned SharePoint as more than just a document management system. It became a versatile platform capable of supporting a wide range of business processes and applications. This shift attracted a broader user base and set the stage for SharePoint's rapid growth.

SharePoint 2010: Expanding Capabilities

SharePoint 2010, released in May 2010, built on the success of its predecessor with a host of new features and enhancements. This version introduced the SharePoint Foundation, the free version that replaced WSS, and SharePoint Server, which offered advanced features for enterprise users. Key innovations included enhanced social networking capabilities, improved business intelligence tools, and more robust content management features.

One of the standout features of SharePoint 2010 was the introduction of the SharePoint Ribbon, a user interface element borrowed from Microsoft Office applications. The Ribbon made it easier for users to access tools and perform tasks, improving the overall user experience. Additionally, SharePoint 2010 offered better support for mobile devices, reflecting the growing importance of mobile access in the workplace.

The Cloud Era: SharePoint Online and SharePoint 2013

With the advent of cloud computing, Microsoft introduced SharePoint Online as part of its Office 365 suite. SharePoint Online provided many of the same features as the on-premises version but with the added benefits of cloud hosting, such as reduced infrastructure costs and easier scalability. This move to the cloud was a game-changer, making SharePoint more accessible to small and medium-sized businesses that lacked the resources to maintain on-premises servers.

SharePoint 2013, released in October 2012, continued to build on the platform's strengths. This version focused on improving social features, such as newsfeeds and community sites, and enhancing search capabilities with the integration of FAST Search. SharePoint 2013 also introduced new development tools, such as the SharePoint App Model, which allowed developers to create custom apps that could be deployed on SharePoint sites.

Modern SharePoint: 2016, 2019, and SharePoint Online

The release of SharePoint 2016 in May 2016 marked another step forward, emphasizing hybrid deployments that allowed organizations to integrate their on-premises SharePoint environments with SharePoint Online. This hybrid approach provided greater flexibility and facilitated a smoother transition to the cloud for many organizations.

SharePoint 2019, released in October 2018, brought further improvements, particularly in terms of the modern user experience. This version introduced modern sites, lists, and libraries, which were designed to be more intuitive and responsive. The modern experience significantly improved usability, making it easier for users to create and manage content.

Throughout these iterations, SharePoint Online continued to evolve as part of Office 365 (now Microsoft 365). The cloud-based version received regular updates, introducing features like Power Automate for workflow automation, PowerApps for custom app development, and integration with Microsoft Teams for enhanced collaboration.

Looking Ahead

As we look to the future, SharePoint's development is poised to continue along the path of innovation and integration. Microsoft's focus on artificial intelligence, machine learning, and advanced analytics is likely to bring new capabilities to SharePoint, further enhancing its value as a comprehensive platform for enterprise content management and collaboration.

In conclusion, the development history of SharePoint is a testament to Microsoft's commitment to evolving the platform to meet the changing needs of businesses. From its humble beginnings as a document management tool to its current status as a powerful, cloud-based collaboration platform, SharePoint has continually adapted to the demands of the modern workplace, ensuring its relevance and utility for years to come.

1.3 SHAREPOINT SUBSCRIPTION AND PURCHASE OPTIONS

Microsoft SharePoint offers various subscription and purchase options to accommodate the diverse needs of businesses, from small enterprises to large corporations. Understanding these options is crucial for organizations looking to leverage SharePoint's capabilities effectively. This section explores the different plans, their features, and the considerations for choosing the right one for your organization.

SharePoint Online Plans

SharePoint Online is a cloud-based service provided as part of the Microsoft 365 suite. It offers several subscription plans, each designed to cater to different business requirements.

SharePoint Online Plan 1

SharePoint Online Plan 1 is an entry-level plan that provides essential features suitable for small to medium-sized businesses. It includes:

- 1 TB of OneDrive storage per user.
- Access to team sites, communication sites, and intranet portals.
- Basic document management and sharing capabilities.
- Integration with Microsoft Office applications.
- Mobile access through the SharePoint mobile app.

This plan is ideal for organizations that need basic collaboration and document management without advanced features.

SharePoint Online Plan 2

SharePoint Online Plan 2 is a more comprehensive plan designed for larger organizations or those with more complex requirements. It includes all the features of Plan 1, plus:

- Unlimited OneDrive storage.
- Advanced data loss prevention (DLP) capabilities.
- Enterprise search and eDiscovery.
- Advanced content management features, including records management and compliance tools.
- Business intelligence tools, such as Power BI integration.

Plan 2 is suitable for businesses that require robust data management, compliance, and business intelligence features.

Office 365 and Microsoft 365 Plans

SharePoint Online is also available as part of broader Office 365 and Microsoft 365 subscription plans, which bundle SharePoint with other productivity tools like Word, Excel, PowerPoint, Outlook, and Teams. These plans include:

Microsoft 365 Business Basic

This plan offers:

- Web and mobile versions of Office apps.
- 1 TB of OneDrive storage per user.

- Access to SharePoint, Exchange, and Teams.
- Business-class email hosting.
- Basic security features.

Microsoft 365 Business Standard

In addition to everything in Business Basic, this plan includes:

- Desktop versions of Office apps.
- Advanced email security features.
- 1 TB of OneDrive storage per user.
- Access to additional Microsoft services like Bookings and Planner.

Microsoft 365 Business Premium

This plan is designed for businesses that require advanced security and device management features. It includes everything in Business Standard, plus:

- Advanced threat protection.
- Device management with Microsoft Intune.
- Azure Information Protection for data security.

Enterprise Plans (E1, E3, E5)

Microsoft 365 Enterprise plans are designed for large organizations and offer the most comprehensive set of features:

- **Microsoft 365 E1**: Includes web and mobile versions of Office apps, email, SharePoint, Teams, and OneDrive.
- **Microsoft 365 E3**: Adds desktop Office apps, advanced security, compliance tools, and analytics.
- **Microsoft 365 E5**: Includes all E3 features, plus advanced security, analytics, and voice capabilities.

SharePoint Server On-Premises

For organizations that prefer or require on-premises solutions, Microsoft offers SharePoint Server. This version allows businesses to host SharePoint on their own servers, providing greater control over data and customization.

SharePoint Server 2019

The latest version of SharePoint Server offers many of the modern features found in SharePoint Online, such as modern sites, lists, and libraries. It also supports hybrid deployments, enabling organizations to integrate their on-premises environment with SharePoint Online.

Licensing for SharePoint Server

SharePoint Server requires a server license for each SharePoint server and client access licenses (CALs) for each user or device accessing the server. There are two types of CALs:

- **Standard CAL**: Provides core SharePoint features like team sites, collaboration tools, and basic content management.
- **Enterprise CAL**: Adds advanced features such as business intelligence, enterprise search, and compliance tools.

Choosing the Right Plan

When choosing a SharePoint subscription or purchase option, consider the following factors:

- **Business Size and Needs**: Smaller businesses with basic needs may find SharePoint Online Plan 1 or Microsoft 365 Business Basic sufficient, while larger organizations may require the advanced features of Plan 2 or Enterprise plans.
- **Budget**: Evaluate the cost of each plan against your budget. Cloud-based plans typically have predictable monthly costs, while on-premises solutions may require a larger upfront investment.
- **Compliance and Security**: If your organization operates in a highly regulated industry, you may need the advanced compliance and security features available in higher-tier plans.
- **Integration**: Consider how SharePoint will integrate with your existing systems and workflows. Office 365 and Microsoft 365 plans offer seamless integration with other Microsoft products, which can enhance productivity and collaboration.

In conclusion, Microsoft offers a range of SharePoint subscription and purchase options to suit different organizational needs and budgets. By carefully assessing your requirements and comparing the features of each plan, you can select the best option to maximize the value of SharePoint for your business.

1.4 UNDERSTANDING SHAREPOINT PRICING

Understanding the pricing of SharePoint is essential for organizations to make informed decisions about adopting and deploying this powerful collaboration platform. SharePoint pricing can be broadly categorized into two main models: SharePoint Online, a cloud-based service included in Microsoft 365 subscriptions,

Understanding the pricing of SharePoint is essential for organizations to make informed decisions about adopting and deploying this powerful collaboration platform. SharePoint pricing can be broadly categorized into two main models: SharePoint Online, a cloud-based service included in Microsoft 365 subscriptions, and SharePoint Server, an on-premises solution. Each model has its own pricing structure, which varies based on features, user needs, and deployment options.

SharePoint Online Pricing

SharePoint Online is available as a standalone service or as part of broader Microsoft 365 plans. The pricing for SharePoint Online is typically based on a per-user, per-month subscription model. Here are the primary options:

SharePoint Online Plan 1

- **Cost**: Approximately $5 per user per month.
- **Features**: Includes basic collaboration tools, 1 TB of OneDrive storage per user, team sites, communication sites, and the ability to access and share documents from anywhere. It also provides mobile access through the SharePoint mobile app.

SharePoint Online Plan 2

Understanding the pricing of SharePoint is essential for organizations to make informed decisions about adopting and deploying this powerful collaboration platform. SharePoint pricing can be broadly categorized into two main models: SharePoint Online, a cloud-based service included in Microsoft 365 subscriptions, and SharePoint Server, an on-premises solution. Each model has its own pricing structure, which varies based on features, user needs, and deployment options.

SharePoint Online Pricing

SharePoint Online is available as a standalone service or as part of broader Microsoft 365 plans. The pricing for SharePoint Online is typically based on a per-user, per-month subscription model. Here are the primary options:

SharePoint Online Plan 1

- **Cost**: Approximately $5 per user per month.
- **Features**: This plan includes basic collaboration tools, 1 TB of OneDrive storage per user, team sites, communication sites, and the ability to access and share documents from anywhere. It also provides mobile access through the SharePoint mobile app.

SharePoint Online Plan 2

- **Cost**: Approximately $10 per user per month.
- **Features**: In addition to everything in Plan 1, Plan 2 offers advanced data loss prevention (DLP) capabilities, unlimited OneDrive storage, enterprise search, eDiscovery, and advanced content management features, including records management and compliance tools.

Microsoft 365 and Office 365 Plans

SharePoint Online is also included in various Microsoft 365 and Office 365 plans, which bundle SharePoint with other productivity tools like Word, Excel, PowerPoint, Outlook, and Teams. These plans vary significantly in terms of features and pricing:

Microsoft 365 Business Basic

- **Cost**: Approximately $6 per user per month.
- **Features**: Provides web and mobile versions of Office apps, 1 TB of OneDrive storage per user, access to SharePoint, Exchange, and Teams, and business-class email hosting.

Microsoft 365 Business Standard

- **Cost**: Approximately $12.50 per user per month.
- **Features**: Includes everything in Business Basic, plus desktop versions of Office apps, advanced email security features, and access to additional

Microsoft services like Bookings and Planner.

Microsoft 365 Business Premium

- **Cost**: Approximately $22 per user per month.
- **Features**: Designed for businesses requiring advanced security and device management features, this plan includes everything in Business Standard, plus advanced threat protection, device management with Microsoft Intune, and Azure Information Protection for data security.

Enterprise Plans (E1, E3, E5)

- **Microsoft 365 E1**: Approximately $10 per user per month. Includes web and mobile versions of Office apps, email, SharePoint, Teams, and OneDrive.
- **Microsoft 365 E3**: Approximately $32 per user per month. Adds desktop Office apps, advanced security, compliance tools, and analytics.
- **Microsoft 365 E5**: Approximately $57 per user per month. Includes all E3 features, plus advanced security, analytics, and voice capabilities.

SharePoint Server On-Premises Pricing

For organizations that prefer or require on-premises solutions, Microsoft offers SharePoint Server. This model requires a different approach to pricing, which includes licensing for both servers and users.

SharePoint Server License

- **Cost**: A one-time purchase cost of around $7,000 per server.
- **Features**: Provides all the capabilities of SharePoint but hosted on the organization's own servers, allowing for greater control and customization.

Client Access Licenses (CALs)

- **Standard CAL**: Approximately $180 per user. Provides core SharePoint features such as team sites, collaboration tools, and basic content management.
- **Enterprise CAL**: Approximately $110 per user. Adds advanced features such as business intelligence, enterprise search, and compliance tools. This is an add-on to the Standard CAL.

Factors to Consider When Choosing a Plan

Business Size and Needs: Smaller businesses with basic needs may find SharePoint Online Plan 1 or Microsoft 365 Business Basic sufficient, while larger organizations with more complex requirements may need the advanced features found in Plan 2 or Enterprise plans.

Budget: Evaluate the cost of each plan against your budget. Cloud-based plans typically have predictable monthly costs, while on-premises solutions may require a larger upfront investment but could be more cost-effective in the long run for certain organizations.

Compliance and Security: If your organization operates in a highly regulated industry, you may need the advanced compliance and security features available in higher-tier plans.

Integration and Scalability: Consider how SharePoint will integrate with your existing systems and workflows. Office 365 and Microsoft 365 plans offer seamless integration with other Microsoft products, which can enhance productivity and collaboration.

Customization Needs: Organizations that require significant customization and control over their SharePoint environment might prefer the on-premises option, despite the higher initial cost and ongoing maintenance requirements.

In conclusion, Microsoft offers a range of SharePoint subscription and purchase options to suit different organizational needs and budgets. By carefully assessing your requirements and comparing the features and costs of each plan, you can select the best option to maximize the value of SharePoint for your business.

1.5 INSTALLATION METHODS FOR SHAREPOINT

Installing SharePoint is a critical step in leveraging its capabilities for collaboration, document management, and process automation. Depending on the deployment model—whether SharePoint Online or SharePoint Server—installation methods and processes vary significantly. This section provides a comprehensive overview of the installation methods for both SharePoint Online and SharePoint Server.

SharePoint Online Installation

SharePoint Online, part of the Microsoft 365 suite, is a cloud-based service, meaning it does not require traditional software installation on local servers. Instead, setting up SharePoint Online involves configuring settings and provisioning sites through the Microsoft 365 admin center. Here are the key steps:

1. **Purchase a Subscription**: Begin by purchasing a SharePoint Online or Microsoft 365 subscription that includes SharePoint Online. Plans vary based on the number of users and the level of features required.
2. **Admin Center Configuration**: After purchasing a subscription, log into the Microsoft 365 admin center. Here, you can configure global settings, such as domain names, user accounts, and overall SharePoint settings.
3. **Create Site Collections**: In SharePoint Online, a site collection is a group of websites under a common top-level site. Use the SharePoint admin center to create and manage site collections. You can create different types of site collections, such as team sites for collaboration or communication sites for broadcasting information.
4. **Assign Permissions**: Configure user permissions to control who can access, edit, and manage content within SharePoint. Permissions can be set at various levels, including site collection, site, and library levels.
5. **Customize Sites**: Customize the look and feel of your SharePoint sites to match your organization's branding. This can include adding logos, customizing themes, and configuring navigation.
6. **Add Content and Apps**: Populate your SharePoint sites with content, such as documents, lists, and libraries. You can also add apps from the SharePoint Store to extend functionality.

The cloud-based nature of SharePoint Online means that Microsoft handles much of the backend infrastructure, including server maintenance, updates, and security. This makes it an attractive option for organizations looking to minimize IT overhead.

SharePoint Server Installation

SharePoint Server is an on-premises solution, meaning it is installed and maintained on your organization's local servers. This method offers greater control and customization but requires more technical expertise and resources. Here's a detailed look at the installation process for SharePoint Server:

1. **System Requirements**: Ensure your hardware and software meet the system requirements for the version of SharePoint Server you plan to install. This typically includes Windows Server, SQL Server, and specific hardware specifications.

2. **Prepare the Environment**: Before installing SharePoint Server, prepare your environment by setting up the necessary infrastructure. This includes:
   - **Active Directory**: Configure Active Directory for user authentication and directory services.
   - **SQL Server**: Install and configure SQL Server to host SharePoint databases.
   - **Windows Server**: Ensure Windows Server is installed and updated on the servers where SharePoint will be installed.
3. **Install SharePoint Prerequisites**: Run the SharePoint Products Preparation Tool to install and configure all the prerequisites required for SharePoint Server, such as IIS, .NET Framework, and other components.
4. **Install SharePoint Server**: Run the SharePoint Server installation wizard. This involves:
   - **Choosing the Installation Type**: Select between a complete server installation or a standalone installation. A complete installation is used for multi-server farm deployments, while a standalone installation is suitable for single-server setups.
   - **Configuring Farm Settings**: If performing a complete installation, configure the SharePoint farm settings, including specifying the configuration database and the farm account.
5. **Run the SharePoint Products Configuration Wizard**: After installation, run the configuration wizard to finalize the setup. This involves creating and configuring the SharePoint farm, services, and web applications.
6. **Create and Configure Service Applications**: Set up service applications such as Search, Managed Metadata, and User Profile Service. These provide various functionalities within SharePoint.
7. **Create Web Applications and Site Collections**: Configure web applications to host your SharePoint sites. Within these web applications, create site collections for organizing your SharePoint sites.
8. **Apply Updates and Patches**: Regularly apply updates and patches to keep your SharePoint Server installation secure and up-to-date.
9. **Configure Backup and Disaster Recovery**: Implement a backup and

disaster recovery strategy to protect your SharePoint data.

Hybrid Deployments

Organizations that want to leverage both SharePoint Online and SharePoint Server can opt for a hybrid deployment. This setup allows seamless integration between on-premises and cloud environments, enabling features like hybrid search, hybrid sites, and hybrid business connectivity services. Setting up a hybrid deployment involves configuring connectivity between your on-premises SharePoint Server farm and SharePoint Online, which requires careful planning and execution.

Conclusion

Choosing the right installation method for SharePoint depends on your organization's needs, resources, and technical expertise. SharePoint Online offers simplicity and ease of management with cloud-based benefits, making it ideal for organizations looking to reduce IT overhead. On the other hand, SharePoint Server provides greater control and customization, suitable for businesses with specific compliance or integration requirements. Understanding the installation process for both options helps ensure a successful SharePoint deployment tailored to your organization's needs.

1.6 THE DESIGN CONCEPT OF SHAREPOINT

The design concept of Microsoft SharePoint is grounded in the principles of collaboration, accessibility, and scalability. As a robust platform for document management and team collaboration, SharePoint's design focuses on creating an intuitive and efficient user experience that meets the diverse needs of modern organizations. This section delves into the core design principles and features that underpin SharePoint, making it a versatile and powerful tool for businesses.

1. User-Centric Design

At the heart of SharePoint's design is the user-centric approach, which emphasizes ease of use and accessibility. SharePoint aims to provide a seamless experience for users, whether they are accessing the platform from a desktop, tablet, or mobile device. The modern SharePoint interface is clean, intuitive, and designed to minimize the learning curve for new users. This user-centric design ensures that employees can quickly find the information they need, collaborate effectively, and contribute to the organization's knowledge base.

2. Collaboration and Teamwork

SharePoint is fundamentally designed to facilitate collaboration and teamwork. It provides various tools and features that enable teams to work together efficiently, regardless of their physical location. Key collaborative features include:

- **Team Sites**: These are dedicated spaces where teams can store documents, manage tasks, and communicate. Each team site can be customized to suit the specific needs of the team, with features like document libraries, calendars, task lists, and discussion boards.
- **Communication Sites**: These sites are designed to broadcast information across the organization. They are ideal for sharing news, announcements, and events, helping to keep everyone informed and engaged.
- **Integration with Microsoft Teams**: SharePoint seamlessly integrates with Microsoft Teams, providing a unified platform for chat, meetings, file sharing, and collaboration. This integration enhances the collaborative capabilities of SharePoint, making it easier for teams to communicate and work together in real time.

3. Document Management

One of SharePoint's core strengths is its comprehensive document management capabilities. The platform is designed to handle vast amounts of documents and data, providing features that ensure documents are organized, secure, and easily accessible. Key document management features include:

- **Document Libraries**: These are specialized lists for storing documents, with built-in version control, metadata, and advanced search capabilities. Document libraries help organizations manage documents efficiently and ensure that employees can quickly find the files they need.
- **Version Control**: SharePoint tracks changes to documents, allowing users to view previous versions, compare changes, and restore earlier versions if necessary. This feature is crucial for maintaining the integrity of documents and ensuring that teams are always working with the most current information.
- **Metadata and Taxonomy**: SharePoint allows users to add metadata to documents, such as tags, categories, and custom properties. This metadata helps to organize documents and improve searchability, making it easier to

manage large collections of files.

4. Customization and Flexibility

SharePoint is designed to be highly customizable, allowing organizations to tailor the platform to their specific needs. This flexibility is achieved through:

- **Web Parts**: These are modular components that can be added to SharePoint pages to provide functionality such as news feeds, calendars, and document libraries. Web parts can be easily added, removed, or configured to create customized pages.
- **Site Templates**: SharePoint offers a variety of site templates for different purposes, such as team sites, project sites, and community sites. These templates provide a starting point for creating new sites and can be customized to meet specific requirements.
- **SharePoint Framework (SPFx)**: This development model allows developers to build custom web parts, extensions, and applications for SharePoint. SPFx supports modern web development standards, making it easier for developers to create rich, interactive experiences.

5. Security and Compliance

Security is a fundamental aspect of SharePoint's design. The platform provides robust security features to protect sensitive information and ensure compliance with regulatory requirements. Key security features include:

- **Granular Permissions**: SharePoint allows administrators to set permissions at various levels, including site, library, folder, and document levels. This granularity ensures that only authorized users can access sensitive information.
- **Data Encryption**: SharePoint uses encryption to protect data both at rest and in transit, ensuring that information remains secure from unauthorized access.
- **Compliance Tools**: SharePoint includes features such as eDiscovery, data loss prevention (DLP), and retention policies to help organizations comply with legal and regulatory requirements. These tools help to manage information lifecycle and ensure that data is handled appropriately.

6. Integration and Extensibility

SharePoint's design concept also emphasizes integration and extensibility. The platform integrates seamlessly with other Microsoft products, such as Office 365, Microsoft Teams, and OneDrive, creating a cohesive ecosystem for productivity and collaboration. Additionally, SharePoint supports integration with third-party applications and services, allowing organizations to extend its functionality and connect with existing systems.

In conclusion, the design concept of SharePoint is built around user-centric principles, robust collaboration tools, comprehensive document management capabilities, customization and flexibility, strong security, and seamless integration. These design elements make SharePoint a powerful and adaptable platform that can meet the diverse needs of modern organizations, fostering collaboration, improving productivity, and ensuring the secure management of information.

1.7 THE SHAREPOINT MINDSET

Adopting SharePoint within an organization involves more than just deploying technology; it requires embracing a particular mindset that aligns with SharePoint's core principles and capabilities. The SharePoint mindset focuses on fostering collaboration, improving productivity, and managing information effectively. This mindset involves understanding how to leverage SharePoint's features to transform business processes and drive organizational success. This section explores the key aspects of the SharePoint mindset and how to cultivate it within your organization.

1. Collaboration and Teamwork

Central to the SharePoint mindset is the emphasis on collaboration and teamwork. SharePoint is designed to break down silos and promote a culture of open communication and shared responsibility. To fully leverage SharePoint's collaborative capabilities, organizations need to:

- **Encourage Open Communication**: Promote the use of SharePoint's communication tools, such as team sites, discussion boards, and newsfeeds, to facilitate transparent and timely communication across teams and departments.
- **Empower Teams**: Give teams the autonomy to create and manage their own SharePoint sites, allowing them to customize their workspace to suit their specific needs and workflows.

- **Foster a Collaborative Culture**: Encourage a culture where sharing knowledge and working together is valued. Recognize and reward collaborative efforts to reinforce the importance of teamwork.

2. Information Management

Effective information management is a cornerstone of the SharePoint mindset. SharePoint provides robust tools for organizing, storing, and retrieving information, but to maximize these tools, organizations must:

- **Establish Clear Taxonomies**: Develop and maintain a clear taxonomy for categorizing and tagging documents. This helps in organizing content logically and enhances searchability.
- **Implement Consistent Metadata Practices**: Use metadata consistently across the organization to improve document management and retrieval. Train users on the importance of metadata and how to apply it correctly.
- **Regularly Review and Update Content**: Establish a process for regularly reviewing and updating content to ensure that information remains accurate, relevant, and up-to-date.

3. Process Automation

SharePoint's capabilities extend beyond collaboration and document management; it also offers powerful tools for automating business processes. To adopt the SharePoint mindset, organizations should:

- **Identify Automatable Processes**: Look for routine, repetitive tasks that can be automated using SharePoint workflows or Microsoft Power Automate. Examples include approval processes, task assignments, and notifications.
- **Design Efficient Workflows**: Create workflows that streamline processes and reduce manual effort. Ensure that workflows are well-documented and easily accessible to users.
- **Monitor and Optimize**: Regularly review automated processes to identify areas for improvement. Use SharePoint's analytics and reporting tools to track performance and make data-driven decisions.

4. Continuous Improvement

The SharePoint mindset is also about continuous improvement and innovation. SharePoint is a dynamic platform that evolves over time, and organizations must be willing to adapt and innovate. This involves:

- **Staying Informed**: Keep up with the latest SharePoint updates, features, and best practices. Subscribe to SharePoint blogs, attend webinars, and participate in user communities.
- **Training and Development**: Invest in ongoing training and development for your users. Provide resources and opportunities for learning to ensure that everyone can use SharePoint effectively.
- **Encouraging Experimentation**: Foster a culture where users feel comfortable experimenting with new features and approaches. Encourage feedback and share successes and lessons learned.

5. User Adoption and Engagement

Ensuring that users adopt and engage with SharePoint is crucial for its success. To achieve high levels of adoption and engagement, organizations should:

- **Communicate Benefits**: Clearly communicate the benefits of SharePoint to users, highlighting how it can make their work easier and more efficient.
- **Provide Support**: Offer robust support for users, including training sessions, user guides, and a helpdesk. Address any issues or concerns promptly to maintain user confidence.
- **Solicit Feedback**: Regularly solicit feedback from users to understand their needs and challenges. Use this feedback to make improvements and tailor SharePoint to better meet their requirements.

6. Security and Compliance

Security and compliance are integral to the SharePoint mindset. Organizations must ensure that data is protected and that regulatory requirements are met. This involves:

- **Implementing Strong Access Controls**: Use SharePoint's granular permission settings to control access to sensitive information. Regularly review and update permissions to ensure they are appropriate.
- **Ensuring Data Protection**: Utilize SharePoint's data encryption and data loss prevention (DLP) features to protect information. Implement regular backups and disaster recovery plans.

- **Maintaining Compliance**: Use SharePoint's compliance tools to ensure that your organization meets legal and regulatory requirements. This includes using eDiscovery, retention policies, and audit logs.

In conclusion, adopting the SharePoint mindset involves embracing collaboration, effective information management, process automation, continuous improvement, user adoption, and security and compliance. By fostering these principles, organizations can maximize the value of SharePoint, transforming the way they work and driving success in today's dynamic business environment.

1.8 THE FUTURE OF SHAREPOINT: TRENDS AND INNOVATIONS

Microsoft SharePoint has consistently evolved to meet the changing needs of businesses and organizations, transforming from a basic document management system to a robust platform for collaboration, communication, and content management. As we look to the future, several trends and innovations are set to shape the evolution of SharePoint, ensuring it remains at the forefront of enterprise technology. This section explores these key trends and innovations, offering insights into how SharePoint will continue to enhance productivity and drive digital transformation.

1. Integration with Microsoft 365 Ecosystem

One of the most significant trends in SharePoint's future is its deepening integration with the broader Microsoft 365 ecosystem. As part of Microsoft 365, SharePoint is seamlessly integrated with other essential tools such as Microsoft Teams, OneDrive, Outlook, and the Office suite. This integration streamlines workflows, enhances collaboration, and provides a unified user experience.

- **Enhanced Collaboration with Microsoft Teams**: SharePoint and Teams are becoming increasingly intertwined, providing a cohesive platform for collaboration. Teams leverages SharePoint for its backend file storage, making it easier for users to access and share documents directly within Teams. Future enhancements will likely include tighter integration, allowing for more seamless transitions between Teams conversations and SharePoint content.

- **Unified Search Experience**: Microsoft Search, integrated across Microsoft 365 services, including SharePoint, aims to provide a consistent and powerful search experience. Users can expect improved search capabilities that leverage artificial intelligence (AI) to deliver more relevant results and insights from across the entire Microsoft 365 ecosystem.

2. Artificial Intelligence and Machine Learning

AI and machine learning are transforming the way users interact with SharePoint, offering smarter and more intuitive experiences. These technologies are being integrated into various aspects of SharePoint to enhance productivity and efficiency.

- **Intelligent Content Management**: AI-driven features such as automated tagging, metadata extraction, and content classification are helping organizations manage their content more effectively. These capabilities reduce the burden of manual data entry and ensure that information is categorized and organized accurately.
- **Personalized Experiences**: Machine learning algorithms analyze user behavior to provide personalized content recommendations and insights. This ensures that users have quick access to the information they need, enhancing productivity and user satisfaction.
- **Advanced Analytics**: AI-powered analytics tools provide deeper insights into how SharePoint is being used within an organization. These insights can help administrators optimize the platform, improve user adoption, and identify areas for enhancement.

3. Enhanced Security and Compliance

As data security and regulatory compliance become increasingly critical, SharePoint is continually evolving to address these challenges. Future enhancements will focus on providing robust security features and compliance tools.

- **Advanced Threat Protection**: SharePoint will integrate more advanced threat protection capabilities to detect and mitigate potential security risks. This includes real-time monitoring, anomaly detection, and automated responses to security incidents.
- **Compliance Management**: SharePoint will offer enhanced tools for managing compliance with industry regulations and standards. This includes improved data loss prevention (DLP) features, eDiscovery, and audit logging to ensure that organizations can meet their compliance obligations.

4. Increased Focus on Mobility and Accessibility

The future of work is increasingly mobile, and SharePoint is evolving to support this trend by providing better mobile and cross-platform experiences.

- **Responsive Design and Mobile Apps**: SharePoint will continue to enhance its mobile applications, providing a seamless experience across devices. Improvements in responsive design will ensure that SharePoint sites are fully functional and user-friendly on smartphones and tablets.

- **Offline Access**: Enhancements in offline access capabilities will allow users to interact with SharePoint content even when they are not connected to the internet. This is particularly important for remote and field workers who need reliable access to information regardless of their location.

5. Low-Code/No-Code Solutions

Empowering users to create custom solutions without extensive coding knowledge is a key focus for SharePoint's future. The platform will continue to integrate with tools like PowerApps and Power Automate, enabling users to build workflows, apps, and automation processes with minimal technical expertise.

- **Citizen Development**: SharePoint will support the rise of citizen developers by providing intuitive tools and templates that enable non-technical users to create custom solutions tailored to their needs. This democratization of app development will accelerate innovation and problem-solving within organizations.

- **Enhanced Integration with Power Platform**: Deeper integration with the Microsoft Power Platform (Power BI, PowerApps, and Power Automate) will allow users to create sophisticated business solutions that leverage data insights, automation, and custom applications.

6. Modern User Experience

The ongoing development of the modern SharePoint experience focuses on providing a more intuitive, visually appealing, and user-friendly interface.

- **Improved Navigation and Layouts**: Future updates will include enhancements to site navigation and page layouts, making it easier for users to find information and navigate through SharePoint sites.

- **Enhanced Communication Tools**: SharePoint will continue to improve its communication features, offering better tools for creating and managing news, announcements, and other internal communications.

The future of SharePoint is bright, with continuous innovations and enhancements aimed at making it a more powerful, flexible, and user-friendly platform. By embracing trends such as AI and machine learning, deep integration with the Microsoft 365 ecosystem, enhanced security and compliance features, a focus on mobility, low-code/no-code solutions, and a modern user experience, SharePoint will continue to be an indispensable tool for organizations looking to drive digital transformation and improve collaboration. As these trends unfold, businesses can look forward to leveraging SharePoint in new and exciting ways, ultimately boosting productivity and achieving their strategic goals.

CHAPTER 2: KEYBOARD SHORTCUTS IN SHAREPOINT

WINDOWS

Frequently used shortcuts

To do this	Press
Navigate the screen.	Tab key
Display the context menu for the selected item.	Shift+F10 or Windows Menu key
Use search.	Alt+S
Copy text.	Ctrl+C
Cut text.	Ctrl+X
Paste text.	Ctrl+V
Undo the latest action.	Ctrl+Z

Work with pages

To do this	Press
Select all text.	Ctrl+A
Insert a link.	Ctrl+K or two left brackets ([[)
Start an ordered list.	1+Period+Spacebar (Number one followed by a full stop and space)
Start a bulleted list.	Minus sign+Spacebar (Minus sign followed by a space)

Navigate a page

To do this	Press
Move between areas and sections.	Tab key
Exit the current operation or close a dialog box or pane.	Esc
Open the selected item.	Enter

To do this	Press
Move between items.	Arrow keys

Undo or redo an action

To do this	Press
Undo the last action.	Ctrl+Z
Redo the last action.	Ctrl+Y

Edit text

To do this	Press
Copy text.	Ctrl+C
Cut text.	Ctrl+X
Paste text.	Ctrl+V
Undo the latest action.	Ctrl+Z
Apply or remove bold formatting.	Ctrl+B
Apply or remove italic formatting.	Ctrl+I
Apply or remove underline formatting.	Ctrl+U
Insert a hyperlink.	Ctrl+K
Delete a selection without adding it to the clipboard.	Delete
Delete the word to the left of the cursor.	Ctrl+Backspace
Delete the word to the right of the cursor.	Ctrl+Delete
Insert a new line (not inside the HTML Paragraph element <P>).	Shift+Enter

Work with lists and libraries

To do this	Press
Display the context menu for the selected item.	Shift+F10 or Windows Menu key
Open and close the **Information/Details** pane.	I

SHAREPOINT ONLINE

Frequently used shortcuts

To do this	Press
Navigate the screen.	Tab key
Create a document.	Alt+N
Upload a document.	Alt+U
Display the context menu for the selected item.	Shift+F10 or the Windows Menu key
Use search.	Alt+S
Sync the library.	Alt+Y
Copy text.	Ctrl+C
Cut text.	Ctrl+X
Paste text.	Ctrl+V
Undo the latest action.	Ctrl+Z

Work with pages

To do this	Press
Navigate the screen.	Tab key
Expand the ribbon or site menus and lists.	Shift+Enter
Move through options in site menus and lists.	Down arrow key or Alt+Down arrow key
Close the open ribbon menu.	Esc
Publish the page.	Alt+B

Edit text

To do this	Press
Copy text.	Ctrl+C
Cut text.	Ctrl+X
Paste text.	Ctrl+V
Undo the latest action.	Ctrl+Z

To do this	Press
Clear formatting.	Ctrl+Spacebar
Apply or remove bold formatting.	Ctrl+B
Apply or remove italic formatting.	Ctrl+I
Apply or remove underline formatting.	Ctrl+U
Left-align the paragraph.	Ctrl+L
Center the paragraph.	Ctrl+E
Right-align the paragraph.	Ctrl+R
Remove the paragraph indent (move the paragraph to the left).	Ctrl+Shift+M
Indent the paragraph.	Ctrl+M
Insert a hyperlink.	Ctrl+K
Delete a selection without adding it to the Clipboard.	Delete
Switch between inserting and overwriting text.	Insert
Delete the word to the left of the cursor.	Ctrl+Backspace
Delete the word to the right of the cursor.	Ctrl+Delete
Insert a new line (not inside the HTML Paragraph element <P>).	Shift+Enter

Work with lists and libraries

To do this	Press
Create a document.	Alt+N
Create a folder.	Alt+N, the Tab key until you reach the **New Folder** button, and then Enter
Upload a document in the **Add a document** dialog box.	Alt+U
Display the context menu for the selected item.	Shift+F10 or the Windows Menu key
Share the selected document or folder.	Alt+S

To do this	Press
Sync the library to a computer or device.	Alt+Y
Open the **More** menu for the selected item.	Alt+M
Open and close the **Information/Details** pane.	I

CHAPTER 3: NAVIGATING THE SHAREPOINT HOME PAGE

The start page is what you see when you login to SharePoint. In SharePoint terms, think of it as your screen that you can change. As your main hub, it makes it easy to get to the tools and resources you use most often and gathers all the important information you need.

HOW TO GET TO THE HOME PAGE

1. Getting into SharePoint: You'll be on the main page of SharePoint when you first log in.
2. It's easy to get to SharePoint. The app launcher is all you need:
- Press the "Start" button on the app.
- From the list, choose SharePoint.

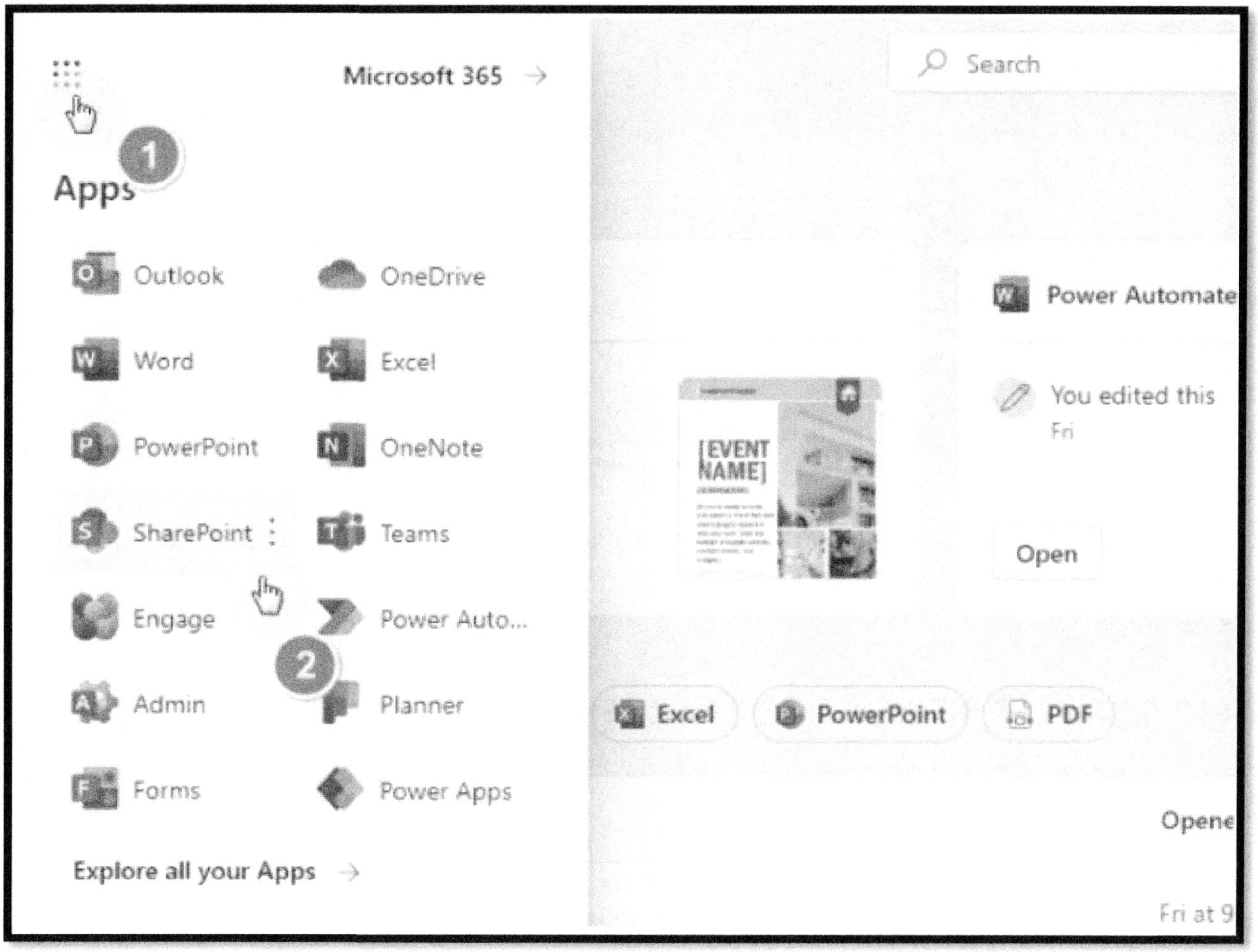

3. By clicking on the house icon;
- You can quickly access the home page from any SharePoint page or site with just one click.
- Below the app menu button, click on the link that looks like a house:

Your ability to access the start page may be impacted by your network access and the permissions your company has granted you. You should talk to your IT staff if you can't get to the start page.

BASIC COMPONENTS OF THE START PAGE

It can be hard to get around the SharePoint Online start page if you're not used to the way it's set up.

But don't worry- it's going to be easy to use once you get the hang of it. The main parts of the start page are shown below. This way you can understand what you're seeing and how to use it properly. In general, this is how the start page looks:

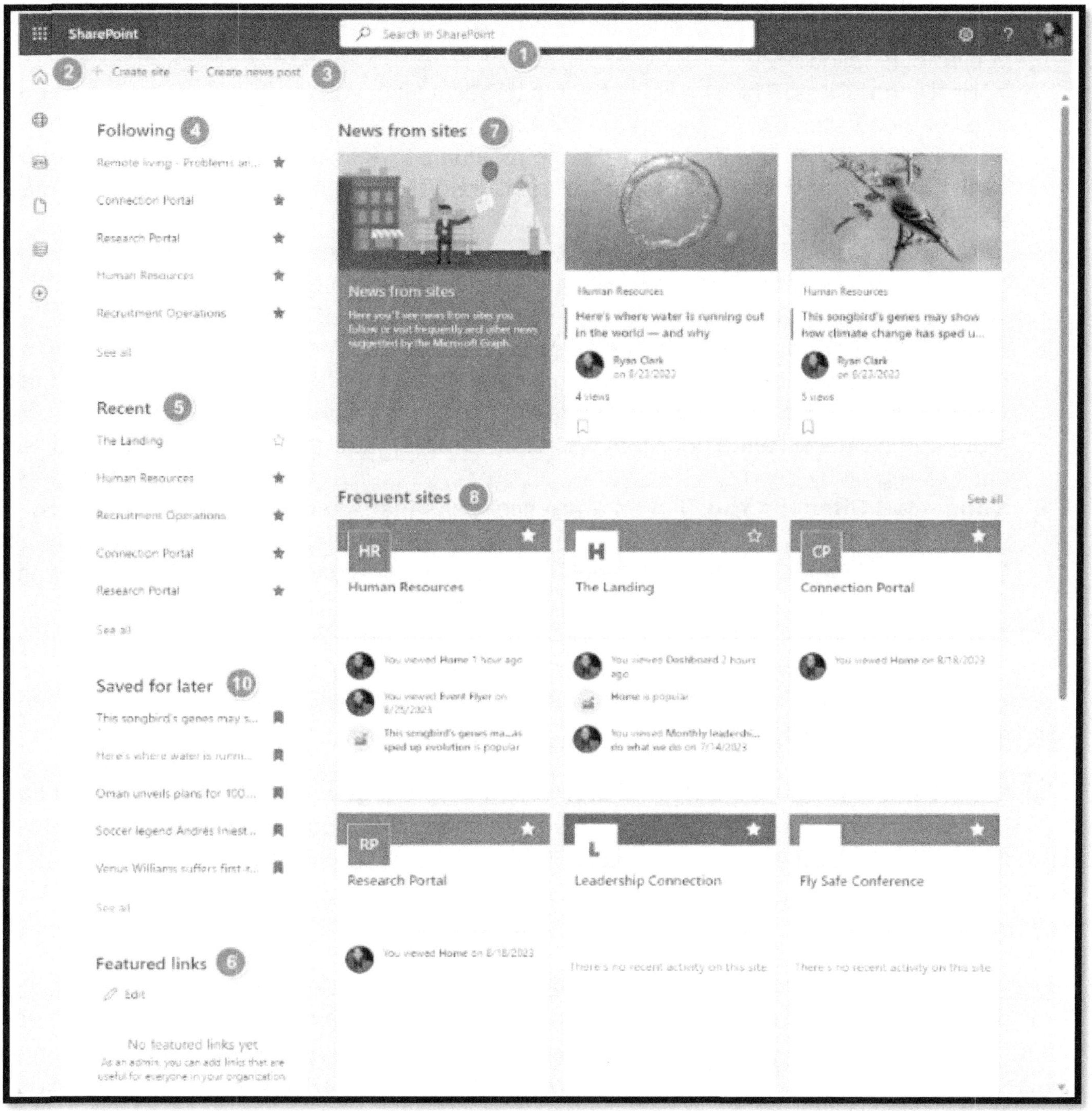

1. **Search:** The search box is right at the top of your start page, which makes it easy to find files and websites you've used lately. No t only that, but it also lets you search for other people in your group, websites, and files. There are search results from OneDrive and other sites that are brought together when you use the search tool on the start page.
2. **Site Creation Feature:** If your boss gives you permission, you will see a button that lets you start making a new site. This will show you a list of choices, and you'll need to pick the type of site you want to make. For example, you could make a news site or a team site.
3. **Post Creation Capability:** Next to the button for making a site is a button for writing new posts, which can be used to share projector team changes. You have to pick which site you want to post the news on since this is done from the home page.

4. **Sites You're Following:** It's easy to get to the sites you've chosen to follow from this section, which lists them all. Click the star icon on the homepage (or start page) of a site you want to follow.
5. **Your Recent Sites:** This is a list of the most recent sites you've visited. You can see a list of all of these sites by clicking on the "see all" link.
6. **Featured Links**: Your company picks the most important sites and websites to show off in this area. People who are managers in Microsoft 365 can change these links to make them more personal.
7. **Latest Site News**: This section shows the most recent news from sites you follow or visit often. The Office Graph makes it easy to show only certain types of news. A see all" link lets you see the 100 newest news stories if there are a lot of them.
8. **Frequently Visited Sites:** This part lists the sites you visit most often and shows you any new action reports for each one. If you visit more than 12 sites often, a "see" link will take you to a full list. It is very helpful to have this tool for quickly getting to Share- Point sites that you use a lot. Remember that Microsoft Graph made this list for you and that you can't change it by hand.
9. **Suggested Sites for You:** T h es e are site ideas that are made just for you based on what you've done and information from Office Graph. Remember that you can only use this feature if the Office Graph settings are right. The Microsoft 365 admin area is where these settings can be changed by administrators.
10. **Saved News Posts:** This is where you can find the news stories you want to read later. You can save a news story to read later by clicking the "pin" icon next to it.

VERSION CONTROL AND CHECK-IN / CHECK-OUT

"Check-in/out" is one of the simplest SharePoint functions that you will likely utilize on a daily basis. You are under no need to uti-lize it. Use caution and only use it when you believe it to be appropriate. The "check-in/out" function in SharePoint is another aspect that might be challenging to comprehend. Even those who constantly check in and out when they don't have to have been seen.

There isn't a single method to discuss the feature, to start. "Check in" is how some refer to it. Some individuals refer to it as "Check out." There are some who say "check-in-and-out," "check-in-out," or the gratifyingly rapid "check-in-check-out." I'm going to substi-tute "check out" for now. But the topic of discussion is the same for all of us. I have no intention of hiding my dislike for check-out. Indeed, "hate" is a powerful word. There's a reason I used it.

In my opinion, check-out is obsolete and unnecessary in a contemporary workplace that makes use of SharePoint 2013, 2016, or Online. Although the concept was sound, most individuals were blind to the little benefits. It added unnecessary complexity to the situation. Yes, it is correct.

HOW TO USE CHECK OUT

To put it simply, checking out is similar to obtaining a tool that guarantees you are the only one who can make changes to a file. Comparable to checking out a book from the library, it belongs to you alone and cannot be altered by anyone else after it is checked out. To have SharePoint check out the file for you, just follow one of the instructions below.

A little green button will appear in the icon's lower right corner after the file has been checked out (item 1 in the photo below). Additionally, SharePoint will notify everyone that the file is checked out to you if you display the "Checked Out To" tab in a library (item 2 in the image below).

Checking the file back in enables you to share it with your colleagues when you've completed editing it. Just shut off the application and save the file one last time. Using the procedures listed below, go back to the SharePoint library and make sure the file is there.

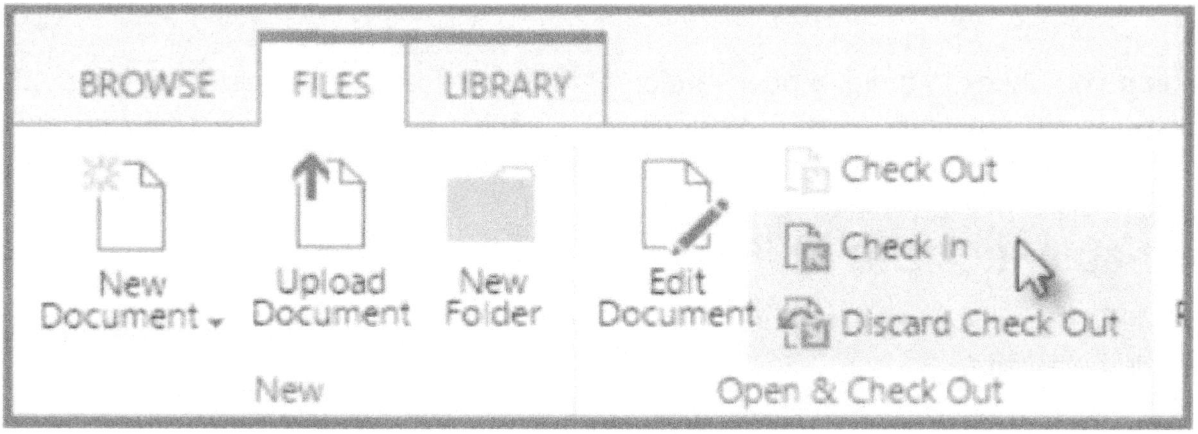

As you can see in that image, you may also remove your check out. Even if you save the modifications, they won't be made again once you check it out. The file will revert to its initial state prior to your inspection. If you make a lot of modifications that you don't want to be utilized, or if the file is broken and you don't want a version created with the broken portions, this is your last-ditch attempt.

Once you designate a file as checked in, SharePoint will ask you whether you wish to maintain the checkout. (I don't get it.)

Even more helpful is the note-taking feature of the pop-up, which allows you to write anything as helpful as "**Finished reviewing**." Now the reader has access to the file. Although I believe notes are a great concept, I don't think anybody really utilizes them. This is probably due to the fact that the option is often only available during file check-in.

Every time you check in a file, a new version of the file is created if versioning is not disabled (Check out is still functional even if versioning is disabled.) This may assist you in creating an updated version of a file-particularly if it isn't an Office file.

REQUIRED CHECK OUT

By default, files in document libraries may be updated without requiring a check-out. If you had to, it would be awful.

By selecting Yes under "Require documents to be checked out before they can be edited?" under **Library settings > Versioning Set- tings**, Site Owners may enforce check-out in a library. Press the "No" button to disable check-out.

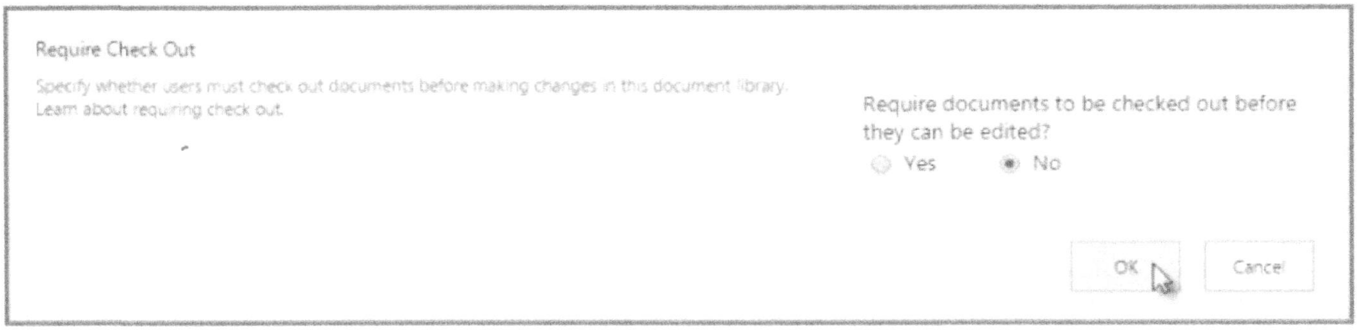

Checkout is often associated with version history; its intended functionality may be inferred from the locations where it is enabled and disabled. Please remember that check-out may only be turned on or off at the library level by the Site Owner alone. It is impossi-ble to complete all of a website's checkout processes at once.

WHEN TO UTILIZE CHECK OUT

When you have rigorous review procedures and want to ensure that no one other than the reviewer may make changes to the file while it's being reviewed, check out might be useful. Additionally, because it's simple for individuals to become lost, every

writer should be well-versed in the checkout process. Unskilled users have the potential to exacerbate the process beyond what is necessary.

Checking it out is another fast and shoddy method to "lock" a file so that no one else may alter it. This may be required for a number of reasons. It will be especially helpful and alluring to those without Site Owner access to the library and the inability to modify permissions. Making a file read-only prevents anybody from editing it and is another method of locking it. The site owner is the only one who can accomplish this.

CHECK OUT AND METADATA

Remember that this section was written for the previous version of SharePoint. This is no longer an issue with the most recent version of SharePoint (in SharePoint Online).

You must check a file before adding it to a library that requires information. This cannot be avoided, yet it is the current state of affairs.

You will be prompted to input the file's details and be presented with your choices if you click the "Upload" button above the menu or library item. Upon completion, the file will be verified.

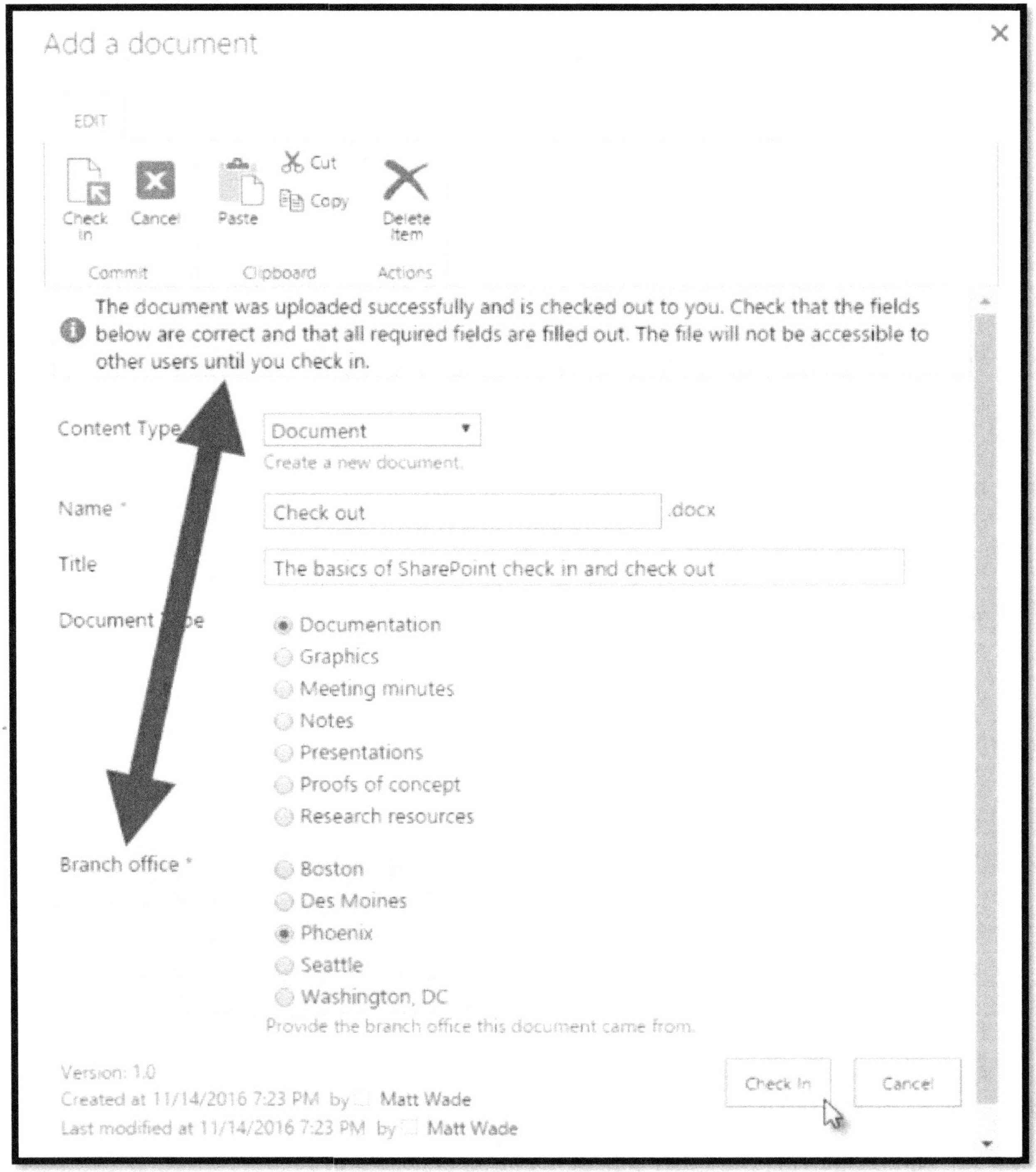

The file or files will upload if you just drag and drop them into your browser (or maybe even use File Explorer). You won't be prompted to choose any options. You checked out the file or files, which is how they ended up in the library. It simply does; it doesn't notify you beforehand.

To add files to a library that requires information, you may either drag & drop them in or use the "upload" option. Make careful to verify that the files were added appropriately after completing either.

In libraries that include the necessary material, I usually advise users to utilize the "upload" option since this procedure may result in a large number of files being checked out and is quite confusing.

CHAPTER 4: ACCESSING SHAREPOINT - WEB AND DESKTOP

OPENING SHAREPOINT VIA WEB BROWSER

Accessing your sites and using the many information and collaboration options that SharePoint offers is simple when you use a web browser to connect to the platform. You can use SharePoint regardless of whether you prefer Internet Explorer, Google Chrome, or Mozilla Firefox since it is designed to function with all major online browsers. For instance, here, we will examine how to access SharePoint on Google Chrome, Mozilla Firefox, and Internet Explorer.

- Launch the web browser.
- In the search field, enter the URL of your SharePoint site. For example, "http s:/ / yoursharepointsite.com".
- Click "Ente r" to open the Linked in website.
- You will be prompted to provide your password details. Please enter your account and password to access SharePoint.

After logging in, you will be able to view all of the tools and content on your SharePoint site.

OPENING SHAREPOINT ON MOBILE DEVICES

Because life moves rapidly these days, having access to SharePoint when you're out and about is essential to being engaged and productive. The increased use of computers and smartphones has led to changes in SharePoint to make it more user-friendly on mobile devices. We will cover the usage of SharePoint on mobile devices, including how to install the SharePoint Mobile App and ac-cess SharePoint using a mobile browser.

INSTALLING SHAREPOINT MOBILE APP

Download the SharePoint Mobile App for iOS and Android smartphones. With a user-friendly style optimized for mobile devices, the SharePoint Mobile App makes it simple to see your SharePoint sites, documents, and lists on your phone. Installing the Share- Point Mobile App on your phone may be done as follows:

- Launch the Google Play Store (Android) or the App Store (iOS) on your phone.
- In the search box, type "SharePoint".
- Locate and tap the official SharePoint Mobile App from Micros oft Corporation.
- To download and install the app on your smartphone, tap the "Get" or "Install" option.
- After the download is complete, launch the SharePoint Mobile App.
- You'll be prompted to log in using your SharePoint account details. Ent er your login information and password to log in.

Because of its mobile-friendly design, the SharePoint Mobile App makes it simple to navigate around your SharePoint sites, read documents, participate in conversations, and collaborate with your team while you're on the road. With full access to SharePoint's capabilities, you may work remotely and maintain connectivity.

USING A MOBILE BROWSER TO ACCESS SHAREPOINT

If you would rather not install the SharePoint Mobile App, you may still visit SharePoint on your phone or tablet using a mobile browser. Here's how to go about it:

- Locate the tablet or phone's web browser.
- Enter the URL of your SharePoint site into the search field. For example, "https://yoursharepointsite.com".
- Click "Ente r" to open the Linked in website.
- If prompted, provide your SharePoint login credentials.

Once signed in, you may access documents, see your SharePoint sites, and perform other tasks just as you would with a desktop browser. The watching experience on the mobile version may vary from that on the PC version since it is optimized for touch inter- actions and smaller displays.

LOGGING IN TO SHAREPOINT

To access and use all of SharePoint's robust features and services, you must first create an account. In this section, we'll go over cre-ating a SharePoint account and changing your password.

ESTABLISHING A MICROSOFT SHAREPOINT ACCOUNT

Creating an account is the first step you should take while using SharePoint. Begin by completing these quick steps to set up your account:

- **Visit the sign-up page for SharePoint:** Go to the SharePoint sign-up page by opening your preferred internet browser.
- Click "**Get started for free**" to proceed. On the sign-up page, there is a free trial option. The process of creating an account will start once you click on it.
- **Enter your email address**: Provide a valid email address that you can be reached at. Messages will be sent to you using this email address, which is connected to your SharePoint account.
- **Type in your personal data.** Simple personal information, such as your name and business name, will be requested by Share-Point. Make sure the information you provide.is accurate in order to complete the registration process.
- **Create a unique password and username.** Create a memorable username and a secure password for your SharePoint account. Make sure your password has a combination of capital and lowercase letters, numbers, and special characters for further security.
- **Accept the guidelines:** After reading the SharePoint terms and conditions, indicate your understanding by checking the box.
- **Check the email address you used**. SharePoint will send a verification email to the address you provided when you've fin-ished registration. Go to your email and click the "Verification " link to substantiate your account.

Fantastic job! The creation of your SharePoint account has been completed. Let's move on to the following subject, which is how to reset your password in the event that you forget it.

RESETTING SHARE POINT PASSWORD

Everyone experiences occasional password forgetting. If you're having trouble accessing your SharePoint account due to forgetting your password, don't panic. In SharePoint, changing your password is simple. To re-enter, do these actions:

- To log into SharePoint, click the following link: Open your web browser and go to the SharePoint login screen.
- On the login page, there will be a password-changing option. Click the "Forgot Password" link to begin the process of recover-ing your password.
- Enter your email address here: Please provide your SharePoint account email address. The email address you used to create the account should be this one.
- Verify your identification: SharePoint will ask you to verify your identity in order to protect your account. This might include
- providing evidence in the form of another document, responding to security questions, or inputting a verification code provided to your email or phone.
- Modify your password: After your identity has been verified, you will be allowed to modify your password. After choosing a new password that satisfies the security requirements, accept the modification.
- To log in, enter your new password. You can now access your SharePoint account with the updated details after changing your password.

Make sure the password you choose is strong and difficult for others to decipher yet simple for you to remember. Try to avoid using everyday language or intimate facts so that others can get to know you right away.

CHAPTER 5: MOBILE ACCESS AND RESPONSIVE DESIGN

UTILIZING MOBILE DEVICES FOR SHAREPOINT ACCESS

To keep in contact with your colleagues and the office, use your mobile phone. You may download the SharePoint app for Apple iOS or Android to access your SharePoint site without using a web browser.

What is conceivable?

Using a tablet or mobile device:

- **Locate SharePoint sites.** This will provide a list of websites that you have been visiting or that the administrators have in- formed you about using Microsoft SharePoint Online.
- **Changing site views:** You may see some of your sites and libraries in SharePoint Online by alternating between the full- screen (commonly known as the PC view) and mobile views. For faster performance, it is recommended to utilize the PC View, particularly when customizing the CSS on your websites.
- **Document Administration:** Check out the most recent documents that have been shared with you, such as those in Word, Excel, PowerPoint, or PDF, and read and distribute them using SharePoint. It is also possible for you to see the documents that you are monitoring in Microsoft SharePoint Online.
- **Navigation:** To go between websites or from one to Microsoft OneDrive for Business, use the menus.

Let's examine the functionality of SharePoint Online on a mobile browser and a mobile application:

SHAREPOINT MOBILE BROWSER INTERFACE

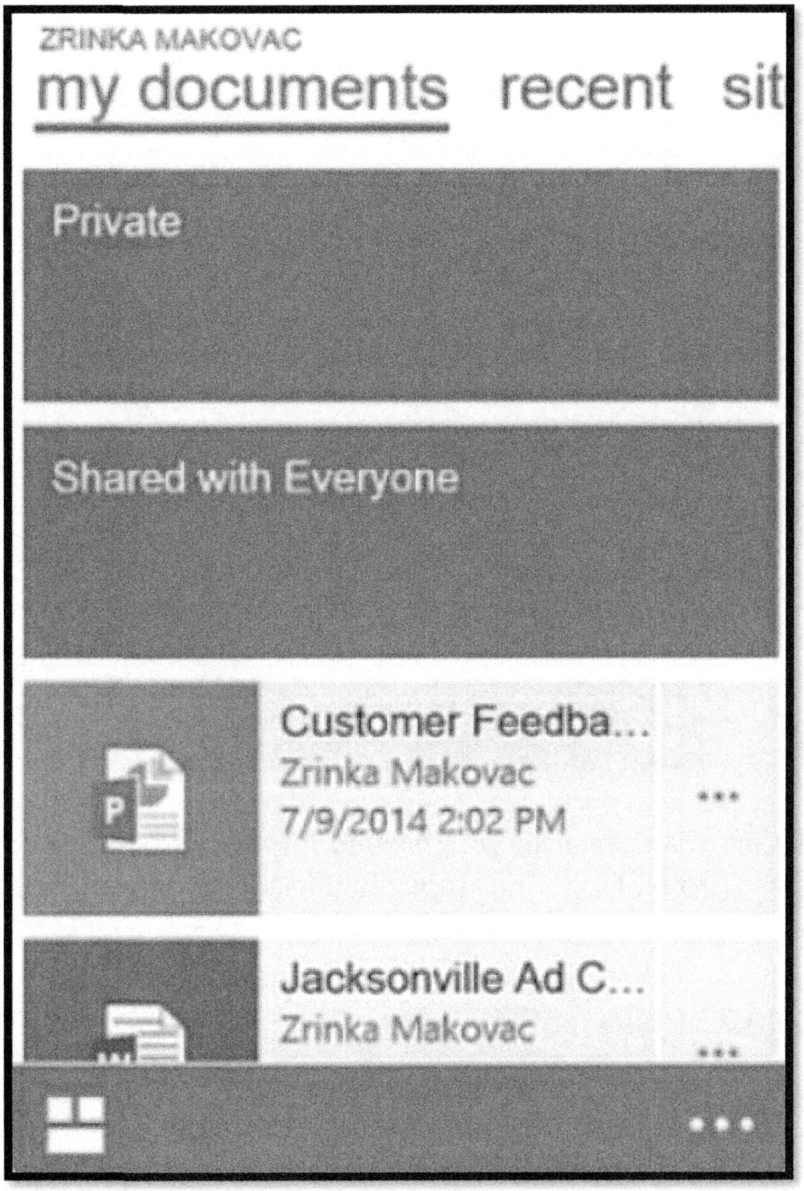

LAUNCH A MICROSOFT SHAREPOINT WEBSITE.

- Open the web browser on your phone.
- In the address bar, enter the SharePoint Online website address (URL).
- As an example, consider SharePoint mydock365. Your URL will feature your domain name instead of mydock365. To log in, use your work or school account.
- Select "Go" located in the lower-left corner of the screen. It's conceivable that in order to see the Go to button, you must press the down arrow(...).
- Select Locations from the list of tiles that allow for movement.

A list of SharePoint sites will appear to you, divided into two groups: sites I'm monitoring and sites that have received pro mot ion. The websites that I follow are more akin to a list of every website you visit.

BROWSING A SHAREPOINT SITE

- From the Sites I'm following or Promoted sites on the Sites page, choose the one you want to visit. Documents and lists are stored in apps, and any subsites are stored in subsites.

By glancing at the name of the view at the top of the page, you may determine which website you are now seeing.

- To open the OneNote notebook for a site, click on the Site Assets tile.
- To see the file on your website, choose the document library that contains it.

OPENING YOUR DOCUMENT LIBRARY IN ONEDRIVE FOR BUSINESS

1. Tap Go in the lower left corner of the screen and choose OneDrive if you are already signed in to a SharePoint site on your PC. The OneDrive for Business app ought to launch.
2. Launch the web browser on your application and follow these instructions if you haven't previously signed in to a SharePoint site:

- In the address bar, type the SharePoint Online website address (URL.) Consider the following URL: http://mydock365.share- point.com. Your URL will include your domain name instead of Contoso.
- Log in using your work or school account (joe@mydock365.onmicrosoft.com,for example).
- Press the Play button in the lower-left corner of the screen. It's conceivable that in order to seethe Go to button, you must press the down arrow(...).
- Select OneDrive from the tile list.

HOW TO SWITCH BETWEEN MOBILE AND FULL-SCREEN VIEW

You may access the full-size view on your PC or phone for your SharePoint sites as well as the OneDrive for Business library.

Toggle between the PC and mobile views.

- a website or library, click the "More" icon in the lower right corner.
- Choose "**Switch to PC view**."

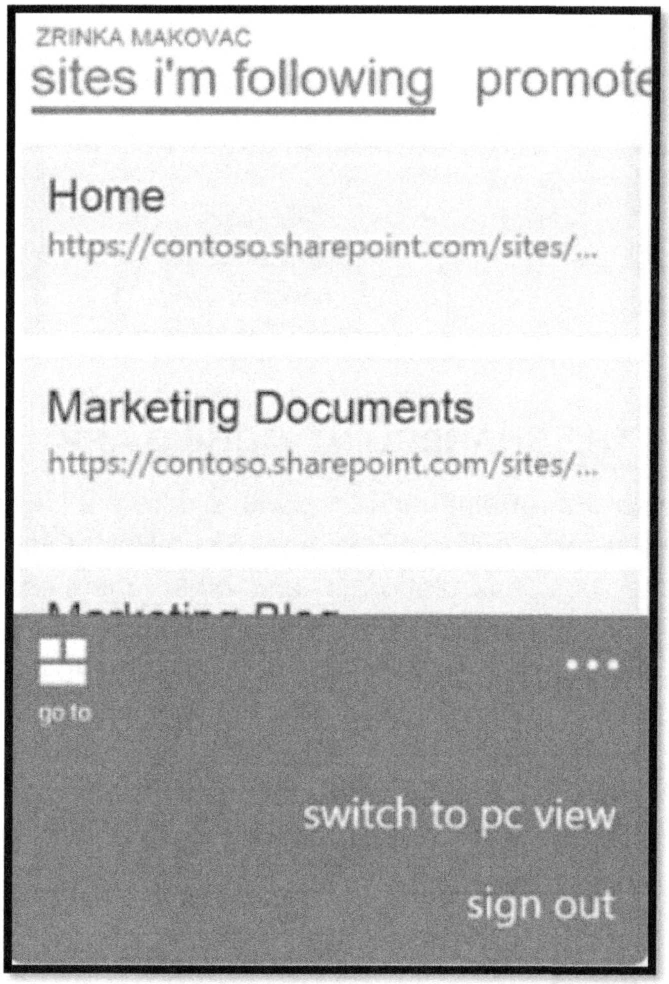

CHANGE THE VIEW FROM PC TO MOBILE.

- Access the SharePoint website and choose Settings from the menu in the top right corner of the screen.

You might not see the setting if you are using a full-screen view. Click the Focus on Content button located next to Edit in the upper right corner of your screen.

- From the Tools menu, choose "Mobile view".

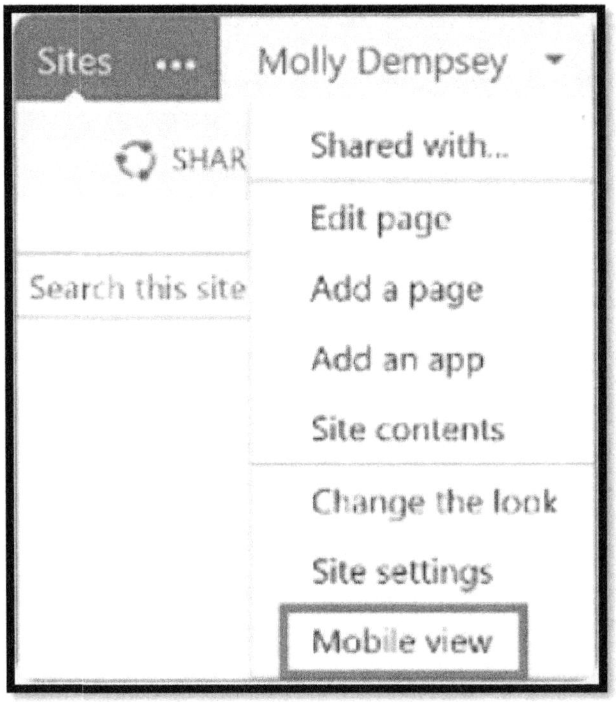

THE INTERFACE OF THE SHAREPOINT MOBILE APP

Are you tired of logging into SharePoint each time with a different URL? You just need to tap to access your intranet when using the SharePoint app. SharePoint lets sales teams keep current on documents, team sites, business platforms, and other users that collab- orate, which is particularly useful for teams that are always on the road. On your SharePoint Team Sites, you may see and edit the SharePoint lists, observe site activity, and rapidly access the most popular or current documents.

To access your SharePoint Online account, you must log in. Multiple accounts may be added, and switching between them fast is possible.

Note: SharePoint Online must already be part of your company's Office 365 subscription in order for this to function.

SharePoint Mobile App: Login Screen and News Feed Interface

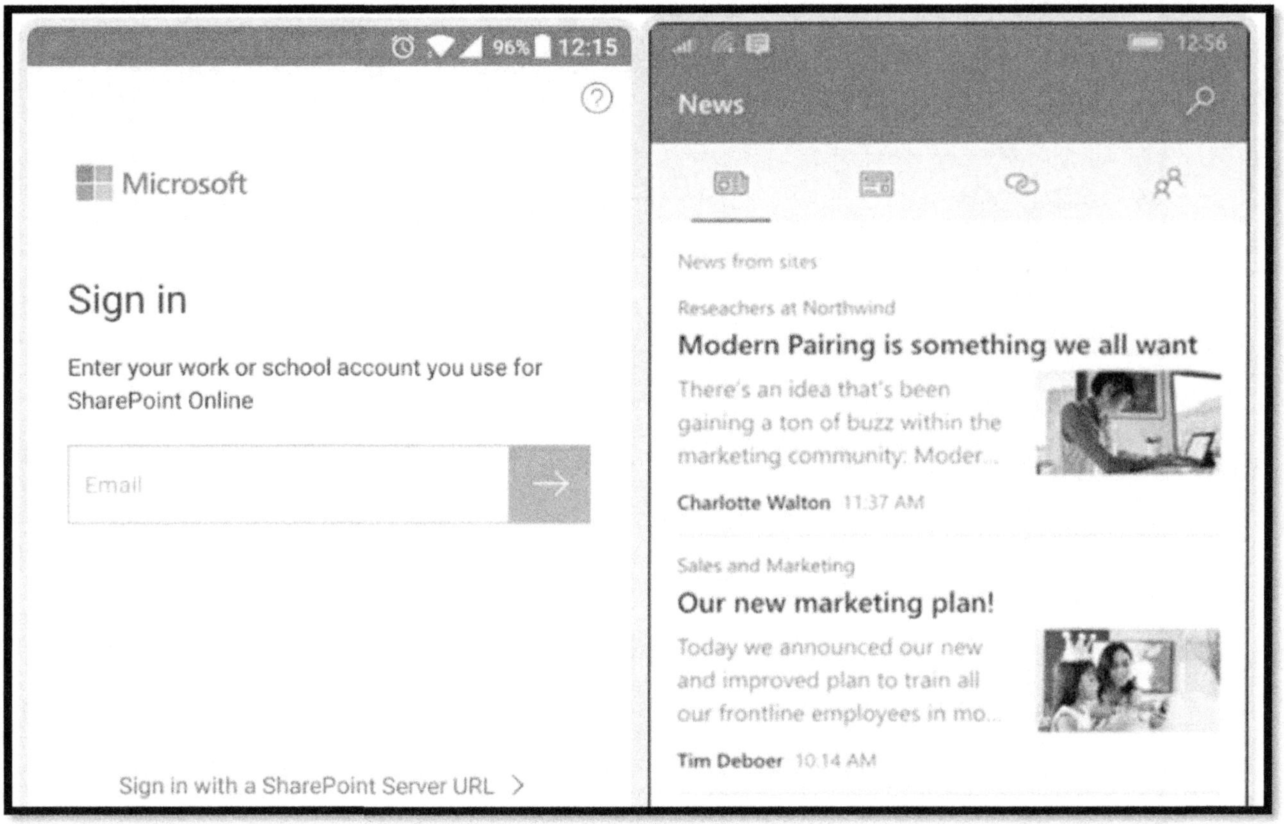

The Search interface in the SharePoint App

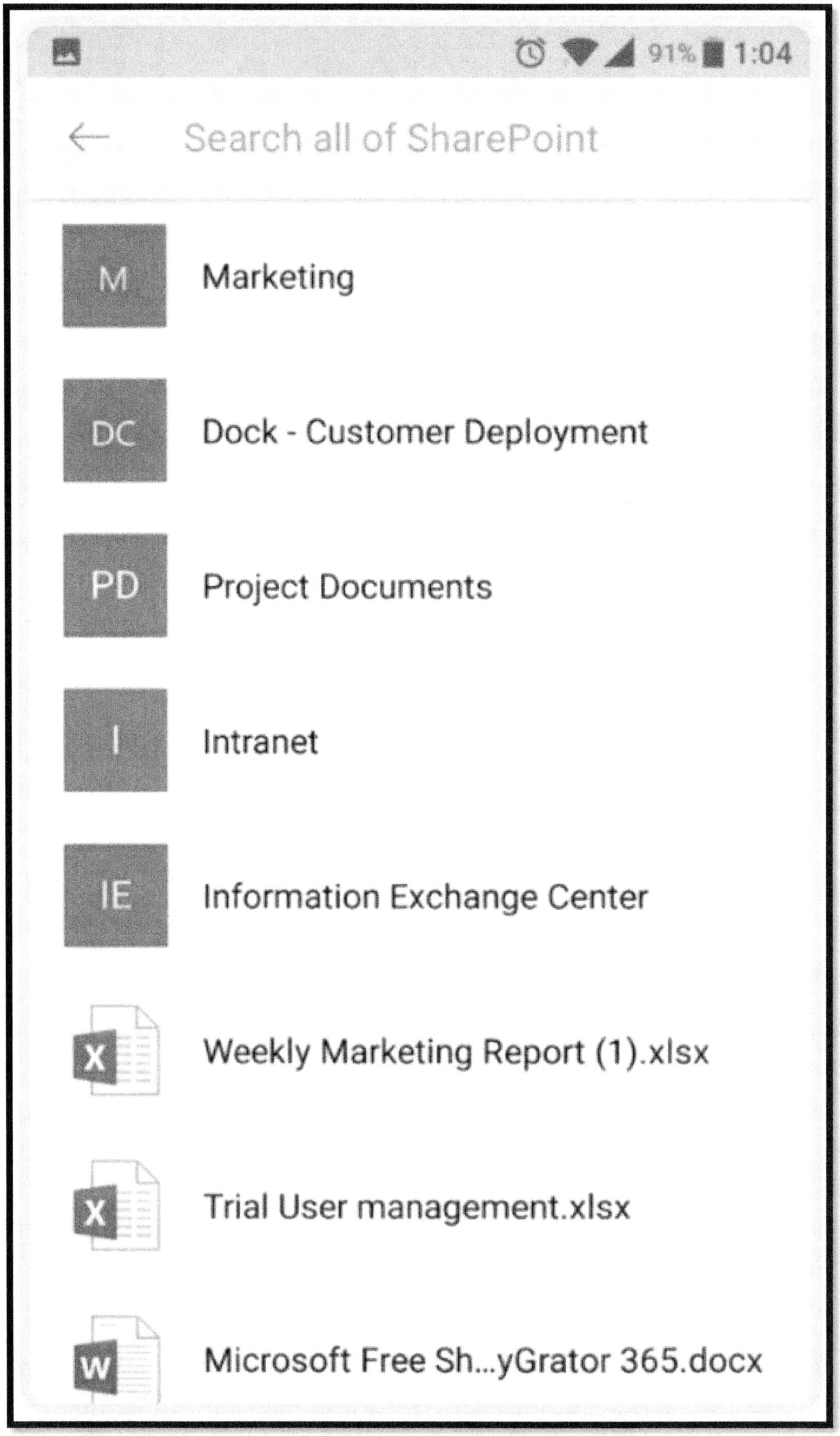

With Enterprise Search integrated into the mobile app, the results are categorized as files, sites, and persons, as shown above.

The Links Tab in the SharePoint Mobile App

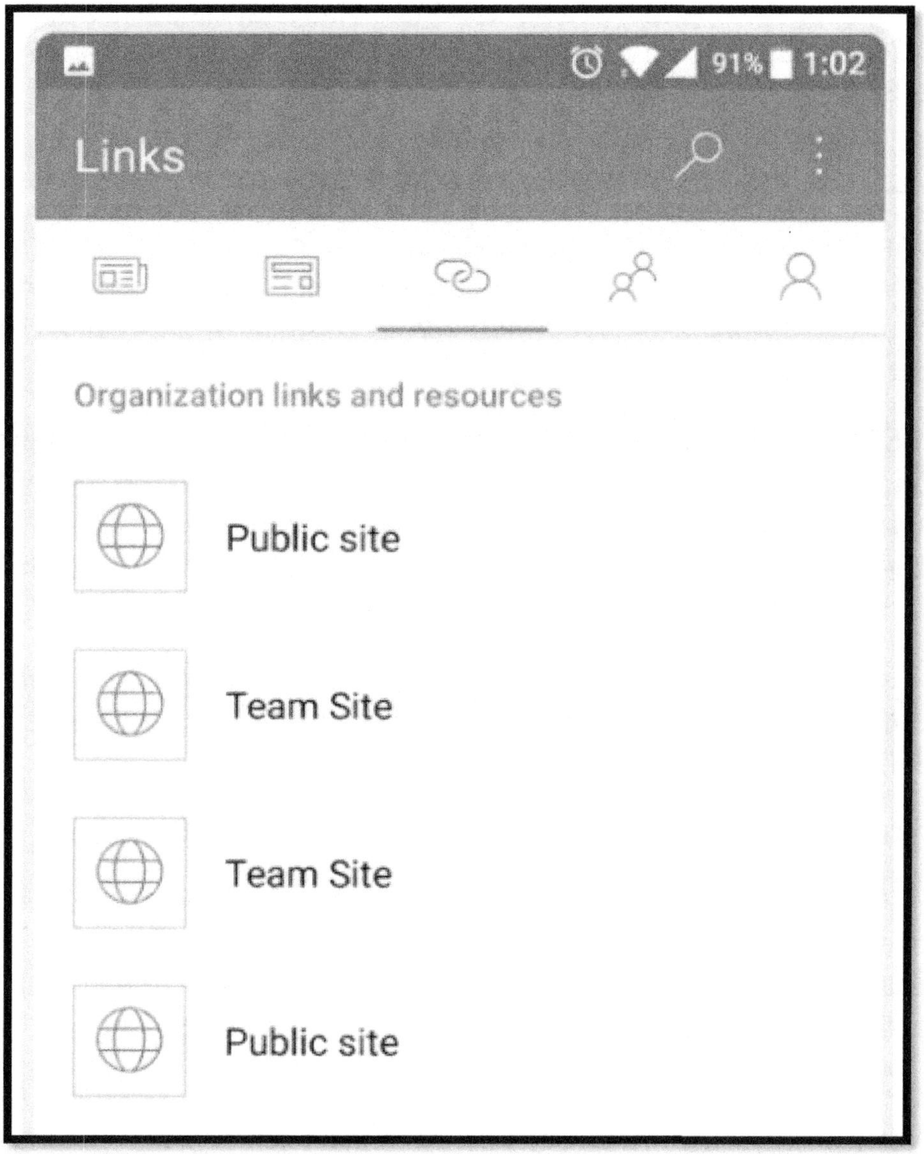

The Links tab is shown in the image. You may discover links here that promote your company. For your employees, this is within the purview of your SharePoint Administrator. These links will assist you in locating the corporate websites and resources that you need.

SUPPORTING THE SHAREPOINT MOBILE APPS ONLINE AND ON-PREMISES

The SharePoint mobile app for iOS, Android, and Windows Mobile allows your SharePoint users to work on their files and data while they're on the road.

These are guidelines that you must follow if you are responsible for an on-premises SharePoint Server farm. Using the SharePoint mobile app, you can:

- Access and work on your sites in Microsoft 365's SharePoint;
- The app is most useful for individuals working on intranet sites while linked to a corporate network. This holds true whether you're using an iOS or Android smartphone or an on-premises SharePoint environment.

COMMON MESSAGES RECEIVED BY USERS

Information on the kind of SSL or TLS certificate or login method being used may be shown to your users or to you when you log in to the SharePoint mobile app. These notifications inform administrators and users about permitted methods to connect Share- Point. The definitions of some of the most often-used terms are as follows:

The unverified SSL certificate that the SharePoint Server is using is incompatible with this application. Additionally, self- signed certificates or certificates issued by an internal Certificate Authority (CA) cannot be used by the SharePoint mo-bile app. You will need an SSL or TLS certificate from a publicly recognized Certificate Authority in order to protect your SharePoint online applications.

This app does not yet support basic authentication, which is used by SharePoint Server. On the other hand, Forms-based identification and NTLM security are supported by the SharePoint mobile app.

Is the SharePoint mobile app responsible for this network traffic?

When iOS and Android devices are connected to SharePoint Server 2016 (on-premises), administrators may see odd data on their network monitors. Visitors to the internet may see inquiry and question-response activity to and from websites such as we-breezi-est-in.cloudapp.net, bn2.vortex.data.microsoft.com.akadns.net, and bl3301-gl drv.com.

These calls are related to data collection and tracking services. Telemetry data is used for analytics purposes, to monitor how Micro- soft 365customers use the services, and to gather fundamental data on the dependability of the services. For instance, OneDrive is available at bl3301-g.ldrv.com, the first URL provided, while Microsoft appears in the domain name of many additional URLs.

Any unusual network data should be reported to the administrators, who should investigate it. Be aware that during this process, you will not be able to disable the SharePoint mobile app's tracking and data-gathering services. You may determine if the Share- Point mobile app is appropriate for your company by reviewing the Privacy Statements.

CHAPTER 6: MASTERING LIBRARIES AND LISTS

ABOUT SHAREPOINT LIBRARIES AND LISTS

Perhaps the two most used components of SharePoint are lists and libraries. Many users of SharePoint will already be familiar with these terms. However, are you aware of their capabilities and how they might expedite your tasks? Here, we'll go into great depth re-garding SharePoint libraries and lists.

A SHAREPOINT LIST: WHAT IS IT?

These files are grouped into lists in SharePoint that are accessible and shareable by all employees in your organization. It is also applicable to other computer components. There are sections and rows, much as in an Excel chart. Excel is a good source of infor-mation for your list.

Lists in SharePoint include calendars, contact lists, and job lists. Yet there are a ton of more uses for SharePoint groups. When creating a data source or a SharePoint list, you may start from scratch. Alternatively, you may choose from the list of themes that Microsoft provides:

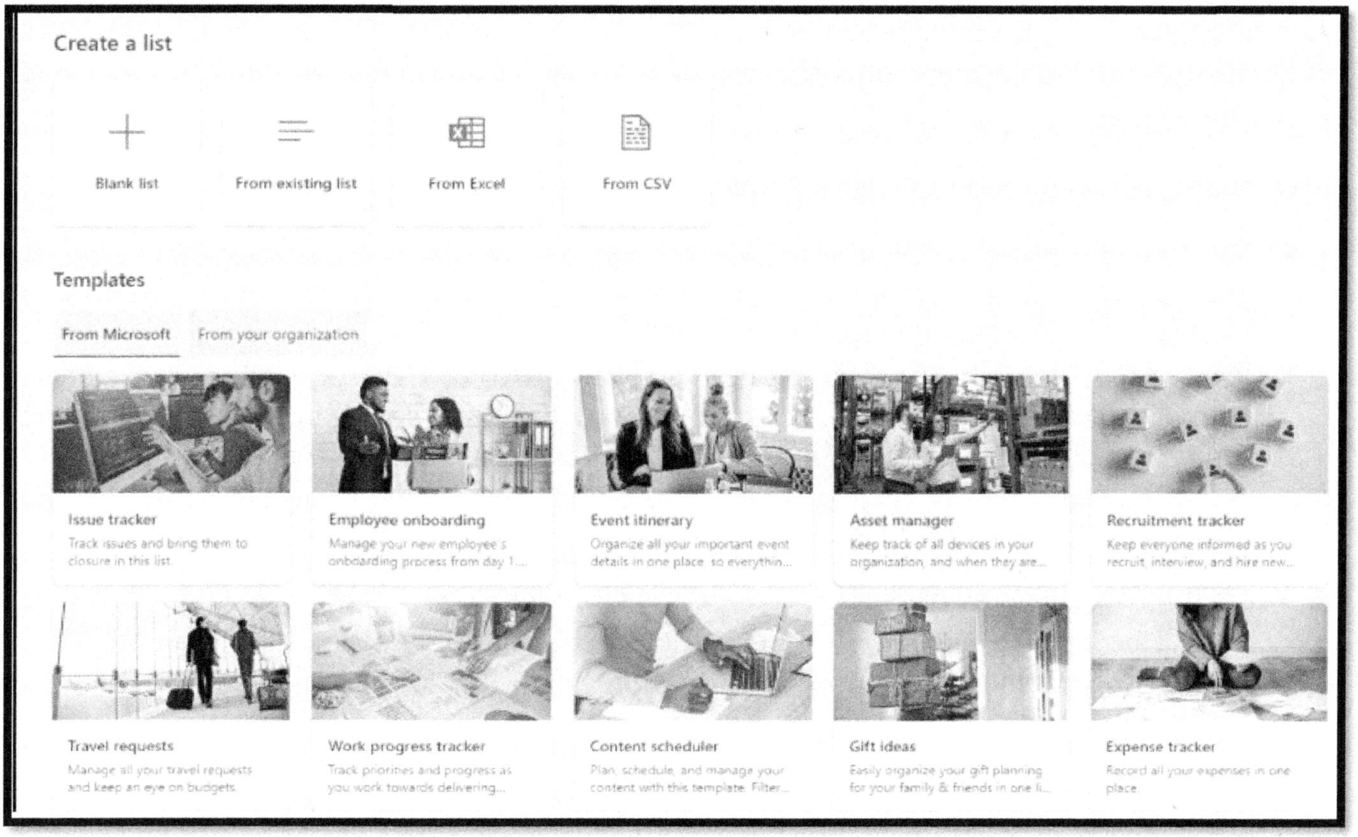

Once you've created it, you may submit files to a list and add or delete columns. You may alter the default view to display the infor-mation in the manner that best suits your needs. The information is significantly simpler to arrange as a result. Even if you are not in the same room with your colleagues, you can still collaborate productively.

Additionally, accessing SharePoint groups is simple on all devices. They expedite and pay close attention to the procedure. Further- more, creating a Power App from a list has never been simpler if you want to automate tasks.

WHAT IS A SHAREPOINT LIBRARY?

SharePoint libraries are also known as document libraries. Document libraries are used by people to store files and other kinds of documents. The word "library" refers to your ability to manage and arrange your information. When you collaborate with your team, versioning makes it simple to stay on top of updates.

The most crucial component of SharePoint folders is the details. Extra details about your files may be found in their metadata. When you add a document to a SharePoint library, you will see its pertinent details. This indicates when and by whom it was up- loaded. You may extend this by adding any further information you believe is necessary. The procedure is the same as in SharePoint when adding fields to a list.

Even for files that are currently open, you may modify the information at any moment. SharePoint lists may even be used to get metadata. It is not necessary to repeatedly add the same details whenever you share a new document.

Your information may be arranged in any way you like in SharePoint files. However, we advise you to make advantage of some rights. Everyone may enter that method; otherwise, things might get more complex.

What distinguishes a SharePoint library from a list?

- **Working together.** In SharePoint Lists, changes may be made immediately. You may check-in and out and compare various versions of a file using SharePoint Libraries. It is now simple to monitor changes as a result.
- **The outcome of the search**. Search results for Word, PDF, and other files stored in SharePoint Lists won't show up. Because they are only files, you are unable to locate them. The primary papers in SharePoint Libraries are always shown first.
- **Modification.** Lists have just major versions, which is the sole distinction between Libraries and SharePoint List s.

Be aware that: While incredibly useful, SharePoint Libraries and Lists do have some limitations. You may not be able to make all the adjustments you would want to since they aren't very flexible. Creating your menu and modifying who can view what, is all included in this. The good news is that up to 30million items can fit inside each one. But don't do that- you don't want to be forced to continue "ever-loading"!

CREATING AND CUSTOMIZING LISTS

Creating a List:

- Open the SharePoint site where the list is to be created.
- Choose "**List**" from the list of possibilities by clicking "**New**".

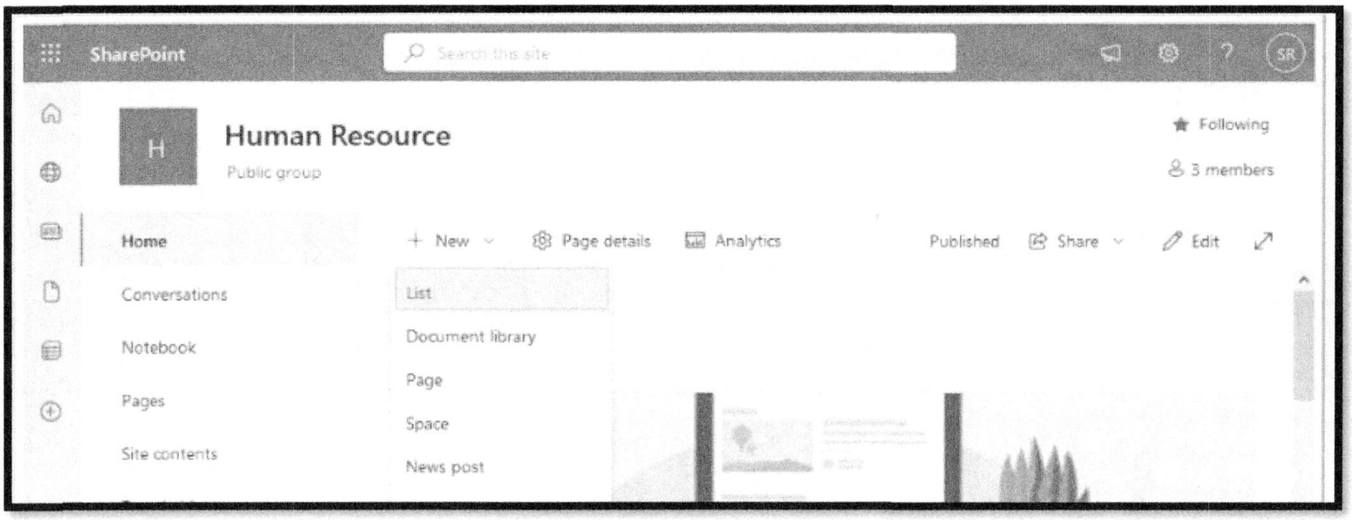

Once you've created your list, you may modify it by adding more columns, entries, and details to the list page.

To ensure that your data is correctly sorted and displayed, make adjustments to your SharePoint List in accordance with your needs.

You have complete control over the modifications you make to your SharePoint List settings. Adding or deleting columns, adjusting column types, and configuring views are a good place to start. Additionally, you may add items to your list by selecting **"New"** and entering the data foreach field before adding the item. You may create a custom SharePoint List that meets your demands by giving you complete control over the structure, site contents, and presentation of your data by beginning with a new list.

Creating a SharePoint List from a Template: List templates for SharePoint provide pre-configured sections and settings for various usage, which streamline the process of creating lists. There are several models available from Microsoft, such as Asset Manager, Content Scheduler, Event Itinerary, Issues Tracker, Recruiting Tracker, and Work Progress Tracker.

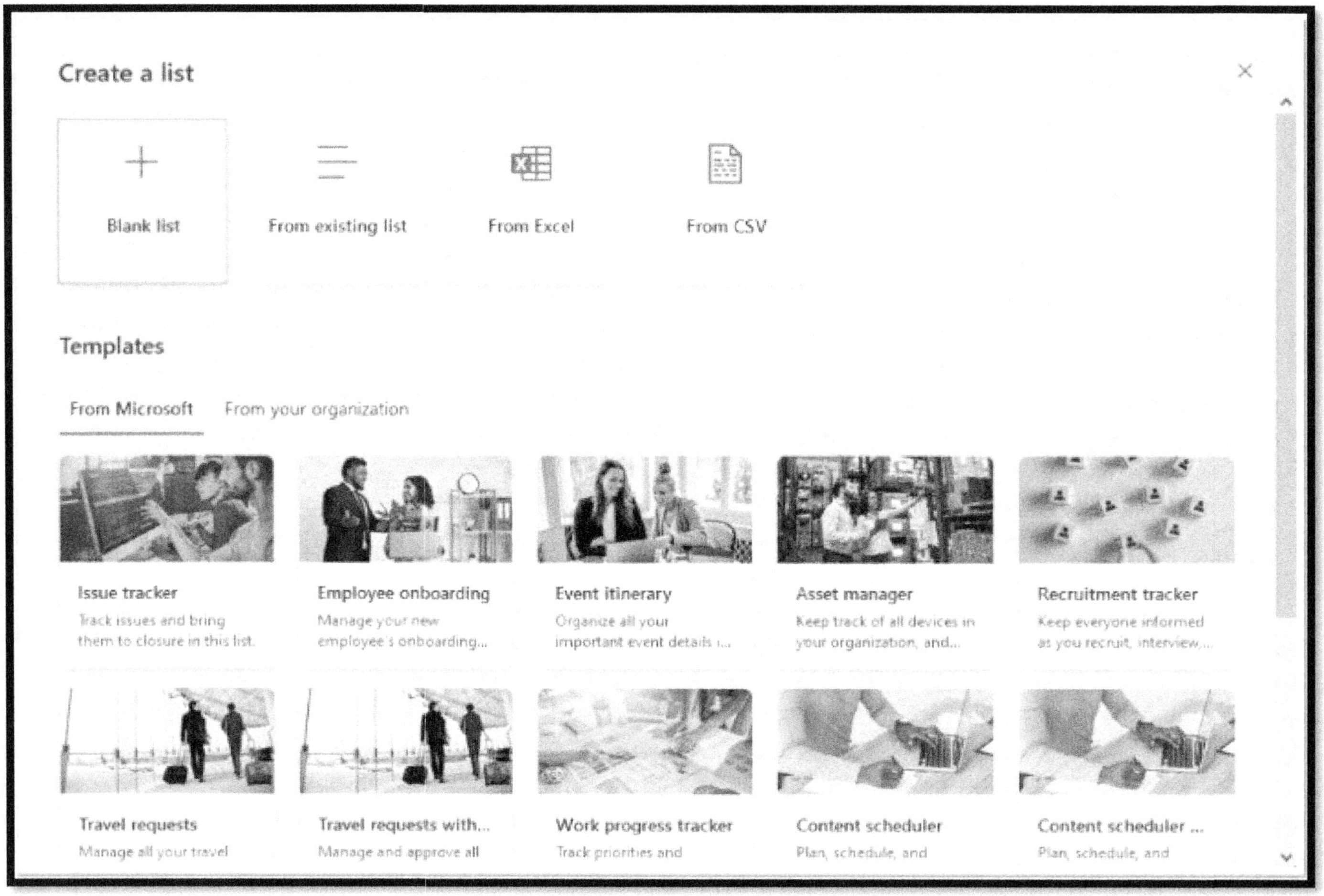

One workable solution is to use data from a Microsoft Excel file to generate an Excel table or a SharePoint list. Nonetheless, an or-derly site information page is necessary for the effective administration of these lists.

Flexibility is essential if the choice is taken to create a personalized list template. This includes the ability to add or remove col-umns, change the kind of columns, and configure views, rules, and processes to tailor the template to individual needs. Using list templates is a great way to take use of SharePoint Lists' customization options while also saving time and effort.

By using pre-existing examples, it is possible to create a SharePoint List quickly and easily without having to start from scratch. This method guarantees a list development procedure that is more simplified and effective.

You can create a SharePoint list similar to this one using a template:

- Go to the page that lists every page on your SharePoint site after opening it.
- Tap or click the "Add an App" icon.
- Select any pre-existing template by clicking on it after selecting the List option.
- Select an existing design that satisfies the requirements in your List.
- Provide any necessary modifications to the List.
- Select "Save" once finished.

SHAREPOINT LIST MANAGEMENT

To manage SharePoint lists effectively, you must customize the lists to meet your company's unique needs. To guarantee optimum operation, this involves the development, configuration, and modification procedures. Establishing rights and access restrictions is also a critical component of list management in order to protect data privacy and improve security measures.

Either the SharePoint web interface or the more complex SharePoint Designer may be used to manipulate SharePoint lists. The latter offers a foundation for more intricate modifications to list forms and procedures. Additionally, users have the option to per-sonalize how their views are displayed, including the ability to filter data by state or sort it by date. Because of its adaptability, users may customize SharePoint Lists to meet their own business requirements.

ADDING COLUMNS TO A LIST

One of the simplest ways to alter the appearance of your SharePoint list is to add fields. In SharePoint, you have the option to create custom fields or choose from a variety of pre-made field kinds, including text, choice, date/time, and more. By adding custom fields, you may get data that is unique to your company's requirements and expedite data input.

This is how a field is added to a list:

- Select the list in which the column is to be included.
- Use the "Settings" button to choose "List settings."
- Once you get to the "Columns" area, choose "Add a column."
- Choose the preferred kind of column and give it a name.
- You can choose to customize other elements, such as the explanation, default number, and column layout, to fit your needs.

In contemporary lists, you may add a new column to the list by clicking the "Add Column "link in the list view.

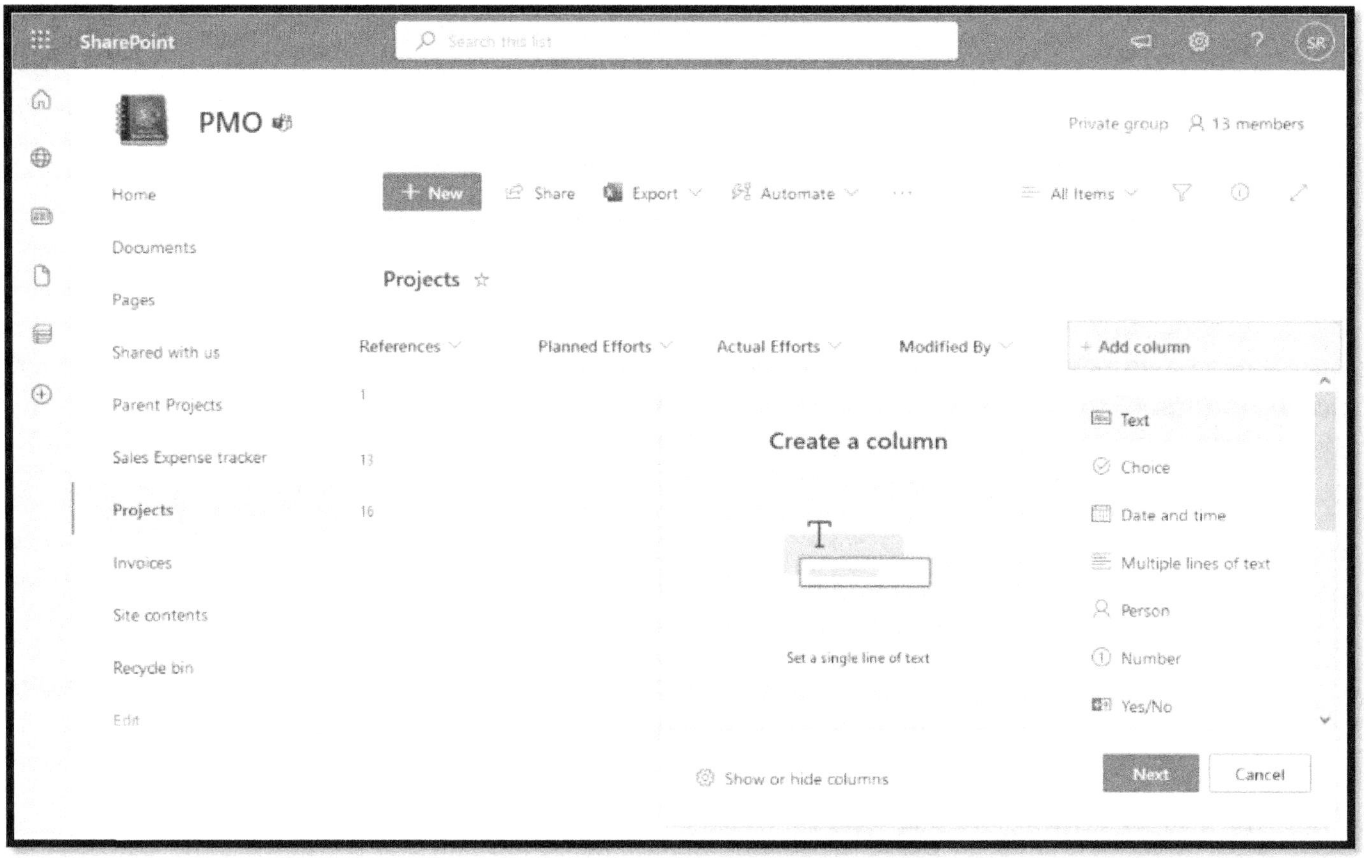

HOW TO REMOVE COLUMNS FROM A SHAREPOINT LIST

Select the column you want to remove from the list settings and press the "Delete" button. It really is that simple. Keep in mind that eliminating a column will eliminate all of the information contained inside it.

ADDING, REMOVING, AND CHANGING ITEMS IN A LIST IN SHAREPOINT

In SharePoint lists, data is stored in items, which are rows of data. Users may add to, modify, or delete items from a list in order to manage the data. One of the simplest methods to manage and arrange online data in SharePoint is by adding items to a list. Users with varying degrees of experience with SharePoint may easily pick up on this method's ease of use. Here's a step-by-step guide on adding items to a SharePoint list:

ADDING ITEMS

- Find the list where you want to add the item by going to your SharePoint Online site or SharePoint server. Get the list open.
- To begin the process of adding a new item, locate the control on the menu and choose "Add new item".
- The form will show up with different fields that match the columns in the list that you set. These fields might be buttons, dropdown lists, text boxes, date pickers, and more.

- Provide correct information in each area. For example, you may enter information about a task in a task list, including its name, summary, deadline, and assignee. To add the item to the list, click" Save". If necessary, at tach files.
- Auto-populate d columns include ID, Created, and Modified.
- Validation rules guarantee data accuracy and conformity to predetermined standards by imposing restrictions on submis-sions or requiring the use of certain forms.

MODIFYING ITEMS

- Select" **Edit Item**" after opening an already-existing item in the list view. The current values for that item will then be loaded when the item form view opens.
- Afterwards, you may alter any word, number, date, and other editable fields as you see fit. Select "Save" to commit the changes to the database.
- Previous iterations may display previous figures and maintain a record of modifications. In the Grid view, you may also mod-ify many list items at once.

ELIMINATING ITEMS:

- Use the checkboxes that are adjacent to the items to choose numerous entries at once.
- Pick one or more items and then pick "Delete."
- As an alternative, you may remove an open item by using the "Delete Item" menu option.
- It is important to remember that objects may only be recovered from backups after they have been destroyed. Use caution to prevent data from being accidentally permanently removed.

The simplest methods for handling individual items in SharePoint lists are as follows. You can maintain the accuracy of your com-pany data in a number of ways by learning how to input, modify, and remove data.

INCLUDING ATTACHMENTS IN A SHAREPOINT LIST

SharePoint Lists allow users to list items and attach supporting documents, giving them access to more information. To add files to a SharePoint list, do the following actions:

1. Go to the particular SharePoint List that has the files you want to include.
2. Decide which desired list item you want to attach files to.
3. To see the attachments box, go to the list item menu and choose the "Attachments" option.
4. From the file list, choose "Attach File."
5. Select the file from your device that you want to attach and press "OK."
6. Repeat steps 4 and 5 if you need to add additional attachments.
7. After you have added all of the appropriate attachments, click "OK" to save the attached files.

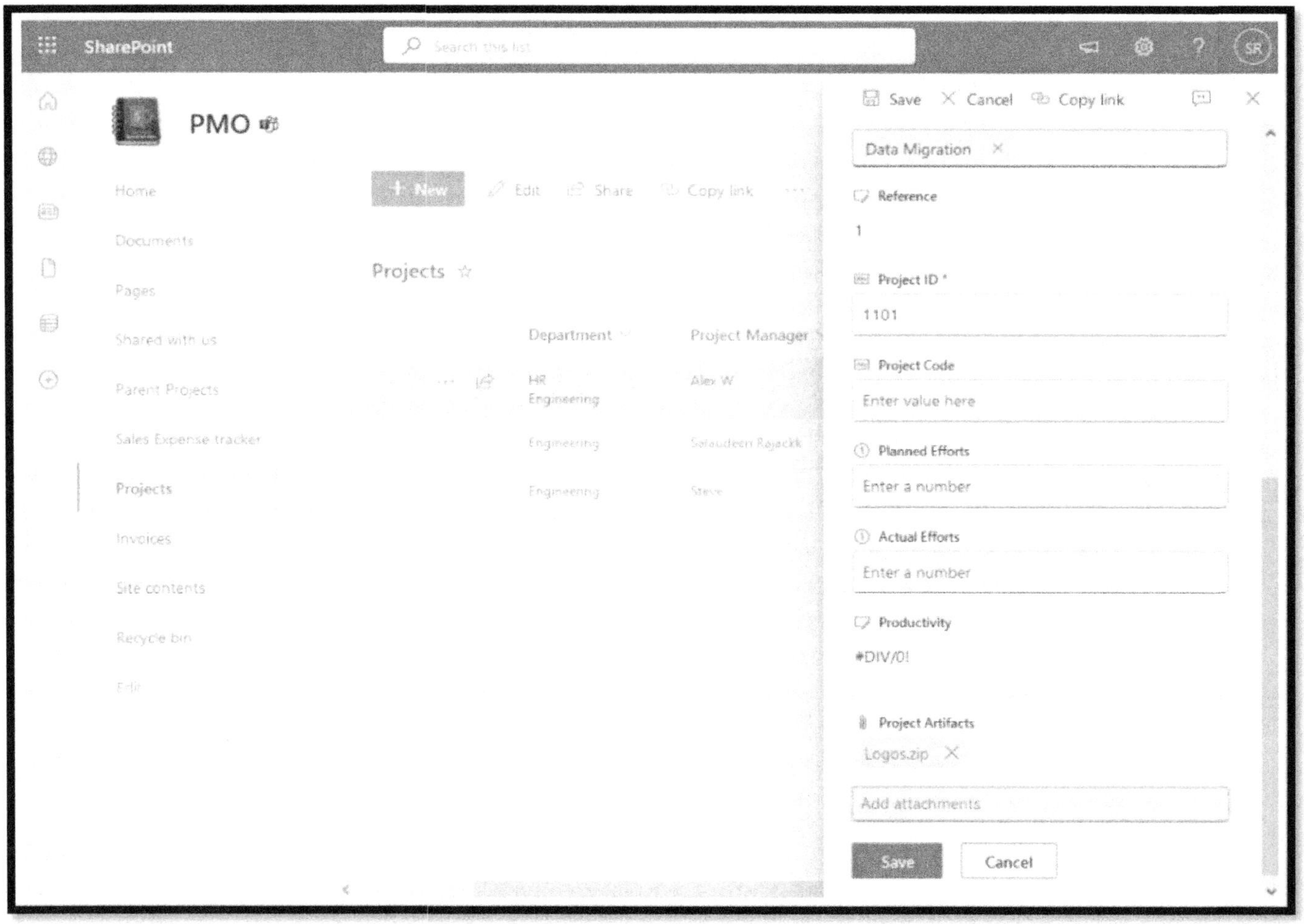

ORGANIZING AND SORTING

1. **Sorting:** Sorting enables you to organize items in a list according to a certain field, such as status, date, or alphabetical order.
- Select the column title you want to sort by and click on it to begin the sorting process.
- Items are sorted in ascending order with a single click and in descending order with a double click.
- Alternatively, to sort the SharePoint List according to a particular attribute, click the filter icon next to the column header.
2. Filtering: Filtering allows you to see things that fit certain criteria, including those that were generated during the previous week or allocated to a certain individual.
- To access filter choices, click the filter icon that is located next to the column header.
- There are several filter choices accessible, such as text, date, and number filters.
- Make use of these filters to focus the information presentation according to your own requirements.

COMPREHENDING PERMISSION LEVELS FOR SHAREPOINT LISTS

With the preset permission levels provided by SharePoint List, you can manage who has access to and can interact with the list. The typical permission levels are as follows:

- **Full Control**: Individuals with this permission level are able to do anything, such as removing the list, changing its settings, and managing permissions.
- **Edit**: Those with the "edit" permission have the ability to add, change, or delete entries from the list. They also have the power to change the settings and layout of the list.
- **Read:** Tose with read permission are able to see the list, but they are not allowed to add or remove items from it.

There are three default groups in SharePoint List, each with different permission levels:

- **Owners:** By default, the Owners group has Full Control, allowing them to change the permissions on the list.
- **Members:** The Members group may modify entries in the list since it has default edit permissions.
- **Visitors:** By default, members of the Visitors group have read permissions, which allow them to see the contents of the list but not edit it.

GRANTING AND REVOKING SHAREPOINT LIST PERMISSIONS

To configure list permissions in SharePoint, follow these steps:

- **Access the list settings:** Navigate to the SharePoint site and choose the desired list. The gear icon labeled "Settings" is located in the top right corner. Select "**Lists settings**" from the menu that displays once you click on it.
- Choose "**Permissions** for this list" option two: On the list settings page, scroll down to "Permissions and Management" and choose the "Permissions for this list" option.
- **Manage permissions**: When you open the list permissions page in SharePoint, you may modify the access granted to indi-vidual users and groups. You may provide permission to individuals or groups, choose the level of authorization (read, contribute, or complete authority), and impose any further restrictions.

CHAPTER 7: MANAGING SHAREPOINT ACCESS

USING SHAREPOINT DISCUSSION BOARDS

SharePoint discussion boards provide an environment for team members to engage in thoughtful discussions, exchange ideas, and solicit feedback from one another. They function similarly to online conference rooms where team members may discuss issues, pose queries, and provide constructive criticism.

The steps to using SharePoint discussion boards are as follows:

- Open the website that has the discussion board you want to create.
- Click the gear icon next to "Settings" and choose "Add an app."
- Search your website for "Discuss ion Board " and click to add it.
- After deciding on a name for the discussion board, choose "New."
- After setting up the discussion board, you may initiate new discussions or join ones that are already underway.
- Select **"New Discussion"** from the menu to start a new discussion.
- Decide on a discussion subject and provide a thorough justification.
- If you want to make it simple to search and locate chats, you may link files or add tags.
- Press the "Post" button to open the discussion to the public.

SharePoint discussion boards encourage cooperation by providing a forum for direct and honest communication. They provide team members the opportunity to voice their opinions, get feedback, and collaborate to find solutions. By using discussion boards, you may aid others by drawing on the expertise and experience of your team, which can enhance teamwork and spark fresh ideas.

SOLVING SHAREPOINT ACCESS PROBLEMS

Although SharePoint is a useful tool for collaboration and document management, like any other piece of technology, it periodically has access issues that make work difficult. In this section, we will examine some typical issues with SharePoint access and discuss some effective solutions.

TYPICAL ERRORS WITH SHAREPOINT ACCESS

- **Error "Access Denied":** The frightening "Access Denied" notice is among the most typical issues when logging into Share- Point. When a person lacks the necessary permissions to read or modify a document or website, this error often occurs. Although it might be inconvenient, there are solutions available.
- **Double-check Permissions:** Verify that the appropriate access has been granted to your user account. If you believe you should have access to a particular document or site, speak with your SharePoint supervisor for assistance.
- **Request entry:** If you lack the necessary permissions, you may directly request entrance from the document or site owner.

  Requesting access to SharePoint is a simple process, and the request's owner may examine it and provide access as necessary.

- **Check the Administrator of the Site Collection.** You may not have adequate privileges at the site collection level if you continue to get "Access Denied" errors even while you are on the main site. Check the work you're doing as a site collection master by getting in touch with your SharePoint supervisor.
- **Error "Page Not Found":** Commonly seen is the "Page Not Foun d" error, usually known as error 404. This error occurs when the requested page or document is not found on the SharePoint site. You may attempt the following fixes to make it right:
  - **Check the website:** Verify the URL again to be sure it points to the desired website or content. A "Page Not Found" error may be readily caused by typos or problematic URLs.
  - **Check Permissions:** You do not have the necessary permissions to see the website or document you wish to view, even if the URL is correct and you continue to get errors. Check your rights and make an admission request if necessary.
  - **Restore Wiped Items:** Occasionally, a page or document may have been inadvertently erased. The "Recycle Bin" in SharePoint is where deleted items may be rediscovered. Check the recycling bin, and replace any items that need to be replaced.
- **"Server Unavailable" Error:** Users may encounter this error while attempting to connect to SharePoint. It seems that the SharePoint server is currently experiencing technical problems based on this notice. Here are some things you can do:
  - **Check the SharePoint Status**: Visit the SharePoint service status page or give your SharePoint administra-tor a call to find out if there are any known server issues or repair activities.
  - **Clear Your Browser's Cache:** Th is may assist in resolving any momentary issues that maybe the source of the "Server Unavailable" message. Simply go into your browser's settings and delete the cookies.
  - **Try a Different Browser:** Try viewing SharePoint using a different browser if the issue persists. There are situations when viewing SharePoint is not available due to issues with certain browsers.

FIXING ISSUES WITH SHAREPOINT ACCESS

- **Speak with the SharePoint Administrator:** See your SharePoint administrator for assistance if you have attempted all of the aforementioned troubleshooting techniques and are still experiencing issues. They are capable and qualified to conduct a more thorough investigation and provide a response.
- **Examine the logs on SharePoint**. SharePoint generates logs that might assist you in identifying access issues. These logs may be viewed by SharePoint administrators to identify error messages or other warning indicators that might aid in troubleshooting.
- **SharePoint Check:** Make sure you are always using the most current updates and patches for SharePoint. Every day, Microsoft releases updates to address known issues and improve system stability. Keeping your SharePoint settings up to date might help prevent entry problems.
- **Do an audit of rights:** Finding any mistakes or misconfigurations that could be blocking access might be aided by doing a rights audit on a regular basis. To ensure that users have the appropriate level of access, check and modify their permis-sions periodically.

BEST PRACTICES FOR SHAREPOINT ACCESS

SharePoint is a feature-rich, powerful platform for document processing and collaboration. To provide a secure and seamless Share- Point experience, it is crucial to adhere to best practices for entry. This section will address two critical aspects of SharePoint access: maintaining security and optimizing its functionality.

SECURING SHAREPOINT ACCESS

The first consideration for SharePoint access should be security. The following is a list of the best techniques to ensure that only authorized users may access your SharePoint site and its functions.

- **User Authentication:** Implement robust security measures to ensure that users who access SharePoint are who they claim to be. Tools like multi-factor authentication, single sign-on systems, and Active Directory integration may help you do this.
- **Role-Based Access Control (RBAC):** This kind of access control enables you to assign varying levels of access and permissions to distinct individuals or groups. The danger of someone else entering without permission is reduced by ensuring that users can only get the tools they need to do their duties.
- **Periodic Access Checks**: Perform periodic access checks to ensure that user privileges are current and appropriate for their roles and responsibilities. For users who no longer need access to certain SharePoint tools, change or delete their permissions.
- **Secure External Sharing:** If you must share SharePoint resources with business partners or others outside your organization, set up secure external sharing capabilities. This might include granting access to visitors, disseminating expiring links, or requiring passwords from outside users.
- **Data Loss Prevention (DLP:)** Establish DLP policies to prevent accidental disclosure or leakage of confidential data. DLP rules may assist SharePoint users in locating and preventing the sharing of sensitive information, such as social security or credit card details.

Check the SharePoint access logs often for any unusual activity or potential security flaws. This may aid in promptly identifying and resolving security-related concerns.

OPTIMIZING SHAREPOINT ACCESS PERFORMANCE

It's not enough to just secure SharePoint access if you want to provide a seamless user experience. You can guarantee that Share- Point operates efficiently and accurately by adhering to these recommended practices.

- **Configure content delivery networks (CDNs).** Send SharePoint content to distant computers by using content delivery net- works (CDNs). This improves the speed and accessibility of SharePoint features, particularly for global users.
- **Turn on Caching:** To keep frequently seen content closer to users, use SharePoint's built-in caching capability. As a result, the SharePoint system responds more quickly and is less busy.

- **Enhance Files and Photos**: Compress and enhance files and photos uploaded to SharePoint in order to reduce their size with- out sacrificing quality. This reduces network traffic and expedites the loading time of SharePoint pages.
- **Use Content Approval:** By establishing content approval procedures for SharePoint libraries, you can ensure that only approved and verified information is published. Preventing inaccurate or missing information from spreading, improves the caliber and reliability of all SharePoint content.
- **Handle Large Lists**: To speed up list views in SharePoint, employ sorting and filters if you have a lot of lists. Using views with selected filters to restrict the quantity of information that users see might also be a smart idea.
- **Routine Maintenance**: Perform routine maintenance tasks, such as database optimization, the deletion of non-used websites or libraries, and the storage of outdated content. This prevents SharePoint from becoming slower over time and main-tains its operating smoothly.

CHAPTER 8: EFFECTIVE COLLABORATION TOOLS

WORKING WITH SHAREPOINT TEAMS AND GROUPS

Three key components of the Microsoft 365 ecosystem that can facilitate better teamwork and communication are Groups, Teams, and SharePoint.

1. **Group** provides a platform for bringing people, discussions, and content together in one location.
2. On **SharePoint,** you can create a shared space where your team can work together on assignments, exchange files, and hold discussions.
3. **Users** can share, save, and organize files with their team using SharePoint. It is a web-based document management and collaboration application. You can create lists, document files, and web pages that are accessible to any member of your team on any device.

On Teams, a chat-based collaboration platform, users can communicate, exchange files, and collaborate on projects in real time with their teams. You can access all of your files and notes from a single location by using Microsoft technologies like OneNote and SharePoint.

These three companies provide your team with a seamless collaborative experience. One can form teams and work with them to coordinate duties. Items related to the team's work can be stored and arranged using SharePoint. You can colla borate on projects, exchange data, and have simultaneous conversations with Teams.

IN WHAT WAY DO THESE SERVICES COMPLEMENT ONE ANOTHER?

Groups, SharePoint, and Teams form a powerful combination of collaboration tools that can improve teamwork. The following are the manner in which these services collaborate:

GROUPS AND SHAREPOINT

You can utilize both Groups and SharePoint to improve teamwork inside your organization. As soon as you create a Group in Share- Point, a site as sociated with the Group is also created. Items that are critical to the Group's work can be stored and arranged on this website.

You can add SharePoint document files, lists, and pages to the Group's SharePoint site, and all Group users will be able to access them. Furthermore, you can limit who has the ability to access, modify, and remove files by using SharePoint permissions. You can monitor the changes made to files over time using version control.

Additionally, SharePoint can be connected to Microsoft Teams, allowing you to access your SharePoint site directly from Teams. Put differently, you can work on files from SharePoint directly in Teams and collaborate with your team on them simultaneously.

TEAMS AND GROUPS

You can collaborate with others in a Group using Microsoft Teams since the software is designed to function effectively with groups.

Creating a new Team also includes the ability to create a Group. This will enable real-time file sharing, discussion, and collaborative work on projects between you and your team members. You can access all of your files and notes from one location by using Teams in conjunction with OneNote, SharePoint, and other Microsoft products.

A new folder is added to the SharePoint site for the Group associated with a newly created Channel in Teams. This indicates that the folder will house all of the chats and data associated with that channel. This helps maintain organization in your job.

TEAMS AND SHAREPOINT

A SharePoint site associated with the newly formed team is also created instantly.

Files that are crucial to the work of your team can be stored and arranged using SharePoint, and you can share those files directly inside Teams. Furthermore, you can limit who has the ability to access, modify, and remove files by using SharePoint permissions. You can monitor the changes made to files over time using version control.

When you add a new Channel, Teams create a new folder on the relevant SharePoint site. This indicates that the folder will house all of the chats and data associated with that channel. It will be simple to keep your job structured as a result.

CREATING AND MANAGING SHAREPOINT TEAMS

With Microsoft Teams, you can collaborate with others by having conversations about tasks or subjects. It can be used to create and manage teams on SharePoint. To collaborate with others, you can make use of the resources associated with each team. SharePoint is the solution for you if you want to create websites, distribute content, and store data.

When you create a new SharePoint site from scratch, it is connected to the new team. A team created by creating a new team from an existing Microsoft 365 group is associated with the SharePoint site that the group is connected to. When you add Teams to an ex-isting SharePoint site, a new team is created and connected to it.

You can learn more about how to integrate Teams and SharePoint, as well as the fundamental terminology and structure, to man- age settings and rights when they are connected. Additionally, you can switch between Teams and SharePoint and understand their differences.

CREATE A MICROSOFT TEAM FROM ASHARE POINT TEAM SITE:

1. Navigate to a group-linked team website that you control.
2. Click **"Add real-time chat"** in the low e r-left corner of the main page of your team site. The **"Add real-time chat"** op-tion can also be found in the **"Next Steps"** panel, which is accessible from your team site's upper right corner.
3. On the page that appears, click **"Add real-time chat"** to learn more about the advantages of integrating Microsoft Teams with SharePoint sites for site owners.

4. To see other choices, click Continue. This will add SharePoint files as tabs in Teams. Select lists, news articles, docu-ment attachments, and SharePoint pages to include in Microsoft Teams. This will enable your staff to collaborate in one area. Remember that the default document library on the team site has already been selected and cannot be al-tered. In the Teams channel, under the Files tab, you will discover this library. Although you can modify your mind, your site's main page will also be selected for you. Select a tool from the Recommended category to see the ones that are most often used on your team site.
5. To create a new Team channel using the tools of your choice as tabs, click "**Add Teams**".

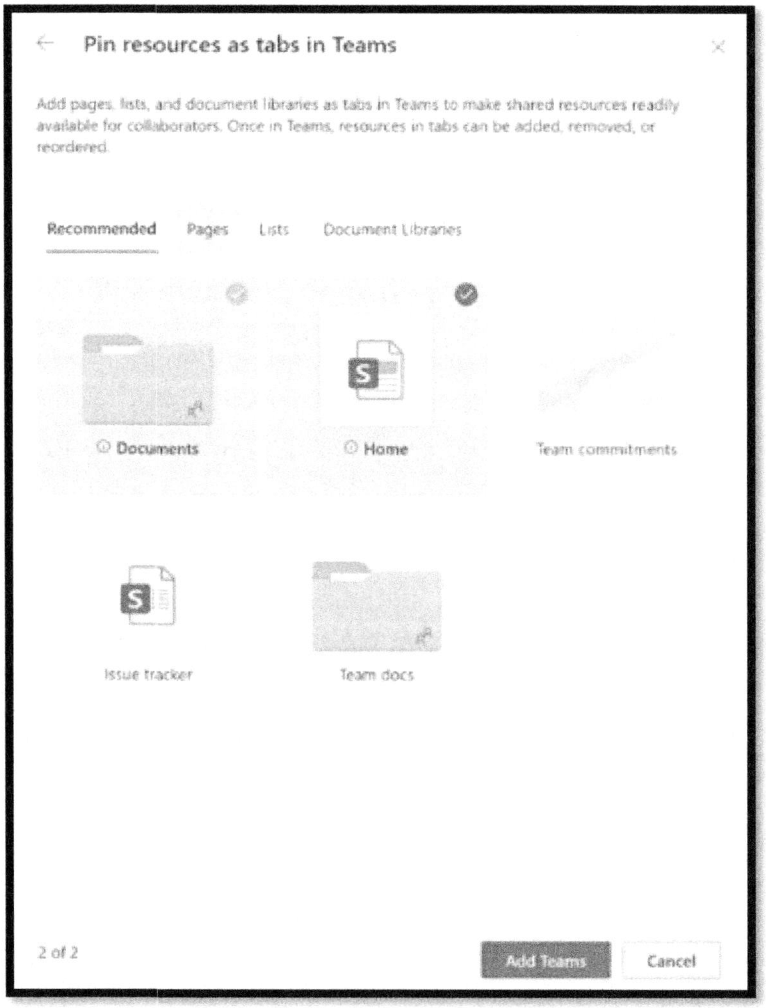

SETTING UP DISCUSSION BOARDS FOR TEAM COMMUNICATION

- Step 1: On the **Microsoft 365 Portal,** click.

Navigate to the "SharePoint" section after opening your Microsoft 365 account.

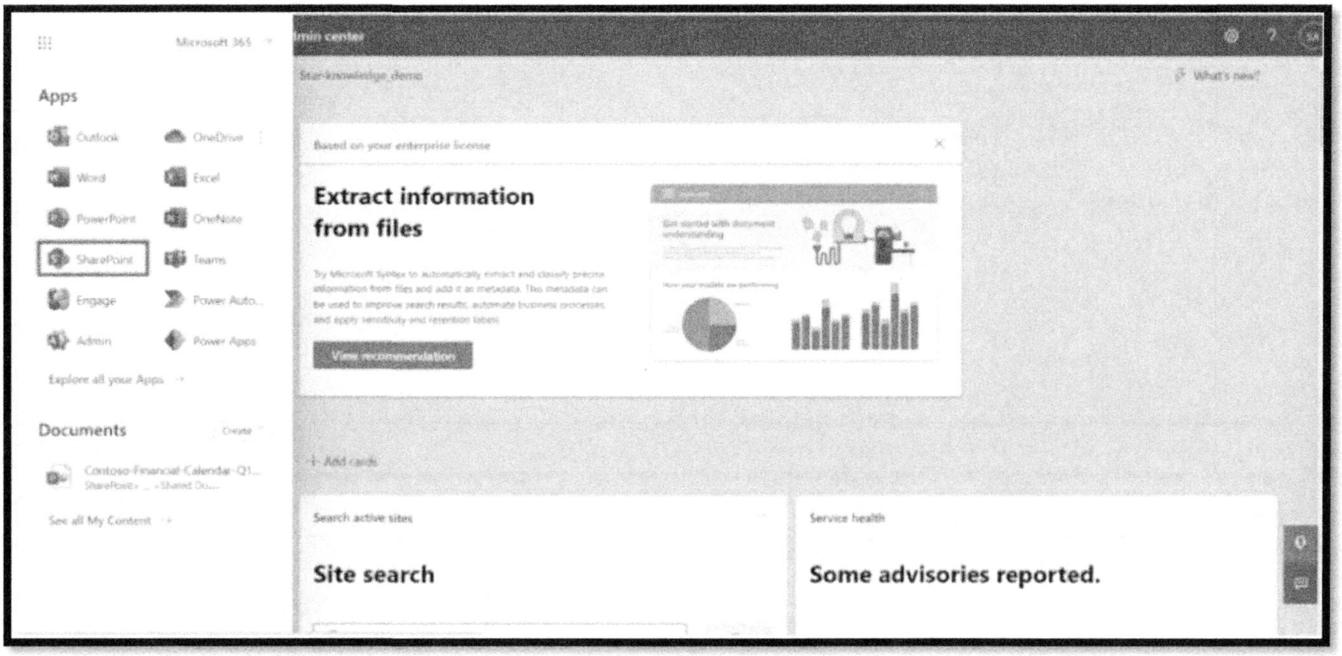

- Step 2: **Add an app**

Navigate to the SharePoint settings, then choose "**Add an App**."

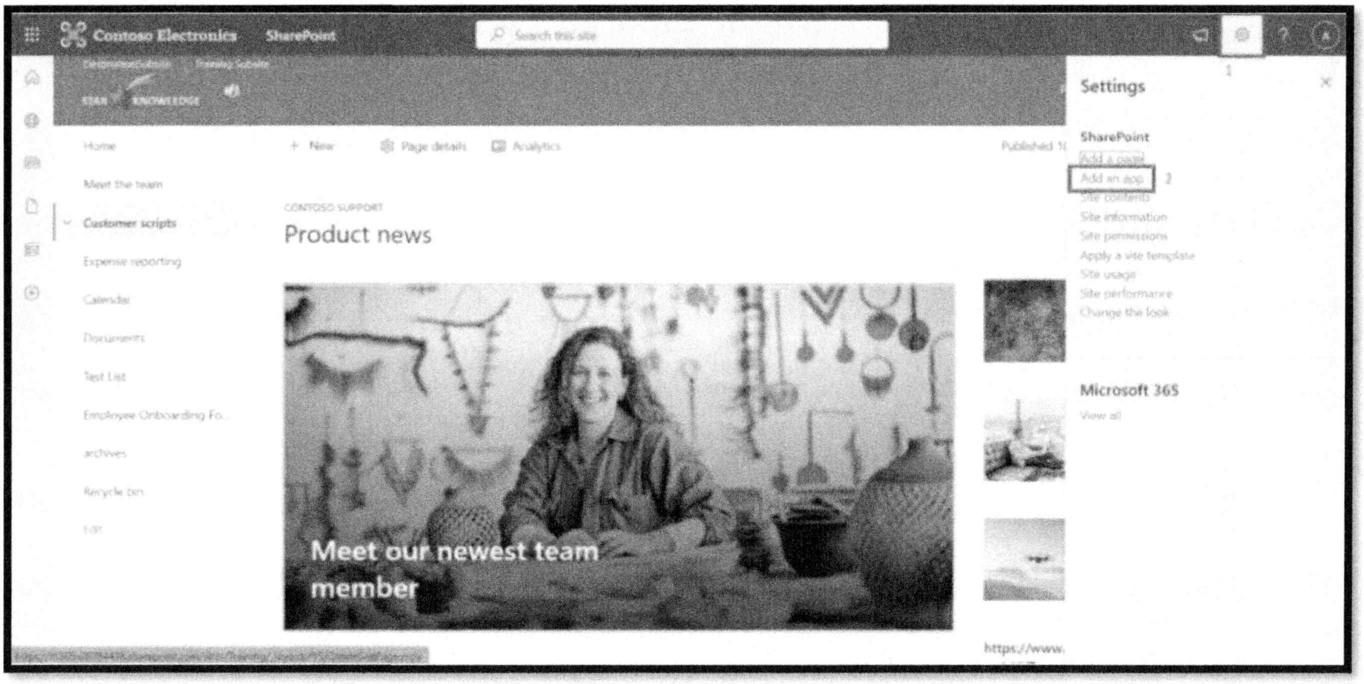

- Step 3: Enable **Classic Experience**

Select "**Classic Experience** " to see the options for the app.

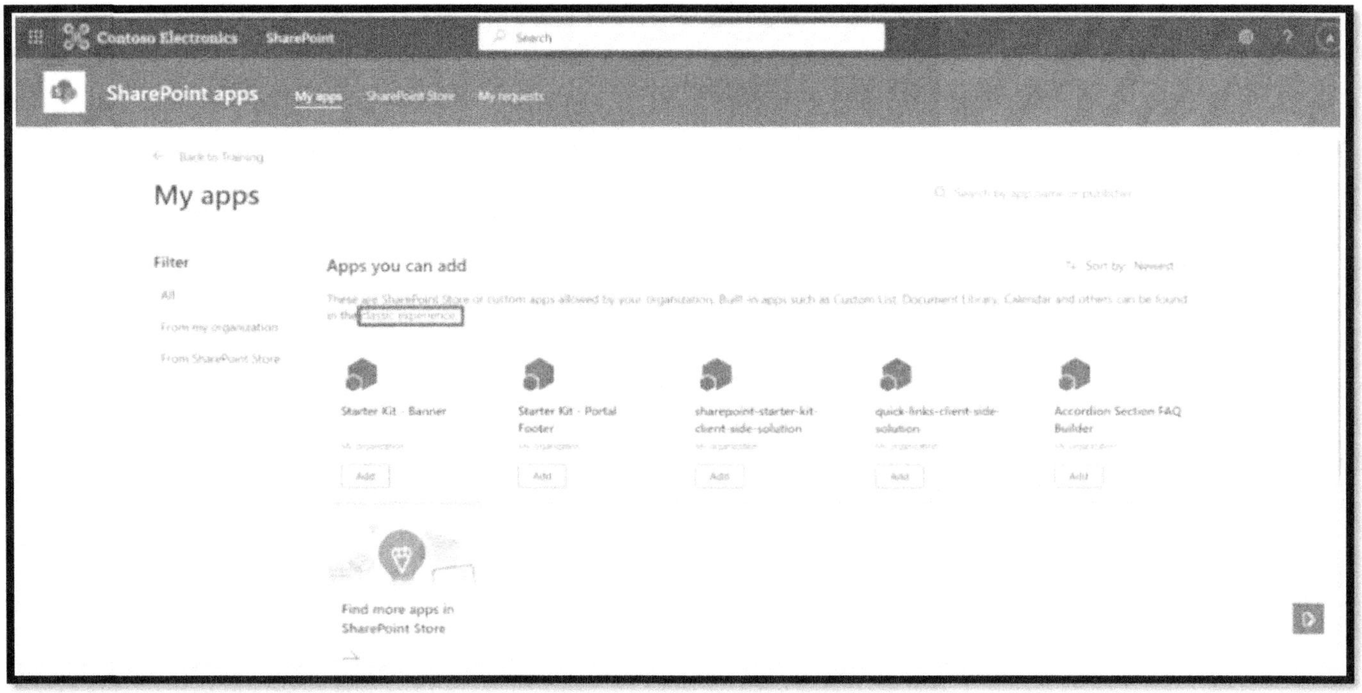

- Step 4: Choose "**Discussion Board**"

Search for "**Discussion Board**" in the Classic Experience app list and choose it.

- Step 5: Supply Board Information

You may either give your discussion board a name or provide a description of its purpose. After that, choose "**Create**."

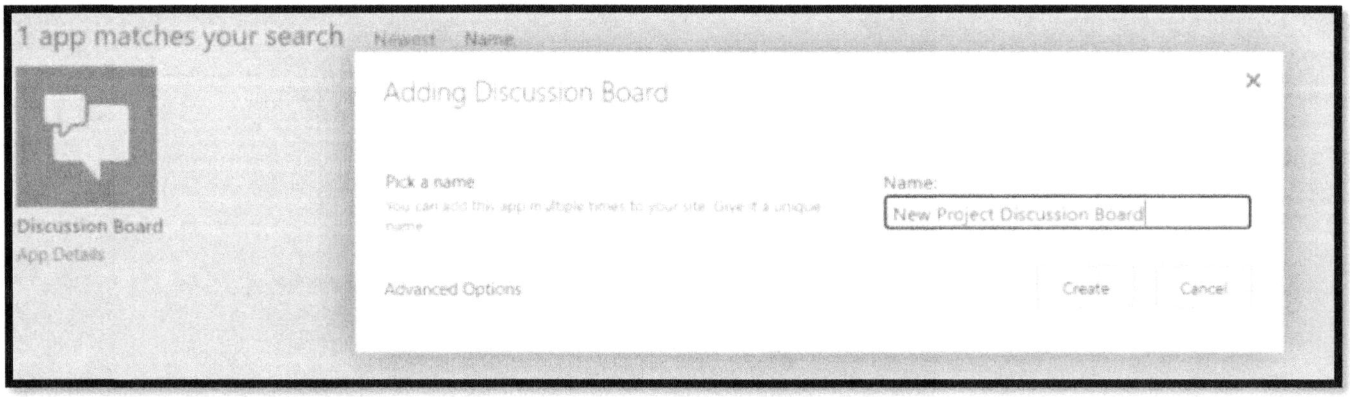

- Step 6: **Go to Your Board**
- **Metadata architecture:** Rules for storage and rule-following, as well as the framework for search and viewing, are all im-pacted by metadata.
- **Search experiences:** The way people "consume" information is designed rather than only perusing it.
- **Personalized Content Experiences:** This refers to the way certain users and user groups are presented with particular content.

Coming up with the ideal layout for hubs, sites, and pages requires sufficient thought. Additionally, knowledge of the topic, the content, design principles, user experience, and Microsoft SharePoint best practices are required. Even with a well-thought-out concept, information design is an ongoing effort. Over time, tasks, individuals, and groups all change. Over time, as you get more understanding of your users, you'll be able to make adjustments that will facilitate finding information.

UNDERSTAND YOUR ROLE AND LEARN HOW TO COLLABORATE

Diverse job types collaborating on an intranet is optimal for the information architecture of your company. For instance, it should be possible for hub owners, IT managers, departmental business owners, and intranet owners to collaborate. Learn more about the roles that each plays in organizing, carrying out, and supervising the information architecture's continuous maintenance.

Organization intranet owner(s): These individuals oversee and manage the overall operations and strategy of your business's intranet. They also make decisions. They are composed of individuals with various occupations. Intranet owners collaborate with IT administrators and business owners (departments) to configure hub-level and global routing. The majority of an organization's intranet administrators' time will be spent organizing and configuring hub-level and global routing.

Departmental business owners: These individuals oversee key divisions within the organization, such as marketing, engineering, and human resources. Within an organization, business unit owners collaborate with intranet owners to ensure that their segment of the business is accurately represented in hub and global navigation. Departmental company owners ought to be engaged early in the planning phase to ensure that the objectives of the business and the users are satisfied.

IT administrators: They put up high-level navigable structures like the start page and hubs in collaboration with the owners of an organization's intranet and the business owners of various divisions. The establishment of guidelines for the creation and usage of websites is another task for ITadministrators.IT administrators aid with the planning, setup, and maintenance of the information design as the organization expands and develops.

Hub owners: They are responsible for the content, branding, rights, and navigational elements of hubs on your company's intranet. Hub owners collaborate with departmental business owners and IT administrators to develop, create, and manage hubs during the course of your company's intranet architecture.

Site Owners: Owners of websites are in control of the rights, access, logos, and material on their websites. If the owner of the hub permits it, site owners can link their sites to hubs. This is dependent upon what the users and company need.

Content Creators: The site's content creators are responsible for posting news and updating the site's content. It should be possible for a content creator to edit sites and pages as a site member. Content writers collaborate with site owners as a team throughout the planning and execution phases.

Content Consumers: Since they do not utilize or see content on any of the three levels of surfing, content consumers are not included in the counts. To ensure that users can locate and use the appropriate material, intranet owners, departmental business owners, hub owners, and site owners should routinely consult with content consumers, particularly during the design stage.

GUIDING PRINCIPLE: THE WORLD IS FLAT

A traditional SharePoint architecture is often constructed using a tiered system of site collections and subsites. Site designs, navigation, and rights are transferred from one site collection to the next. Once constructed, this structure can be inflexible and difficult to maintain. In the latest version of SharePoint, subsites are not recommended. With today's "flat" SharePoint environment, you should plan to create a distinct website for every subject, project, or work unit.

This will enable you to move websites about in your brow sing design without breaking links, and it will also make it simple to share responsibility and management for each group of information. Also, if a subject is no longer required, you can easily terminate or remove a website with little impact.

You can connect websites and content using the following information design technologies in the new flat world:

- To display material from other websites on top of your own, use **"roll up"** web components such as News, Highlighted con- tent, or Sites.
- Provide your reader with further details by including internal links to other resources on the topic (as indicated in the last bullet point).
- Ensure the navigation of your website includes obvious connections to related websites.
- To link relevant groups of websites, use hubs.

LEVELS OF NAVIGATION

Three levels of navigation should be considered while using contemporary SharePoint:

- **Global navigation** for the whole set of websites that make up your intranet
- For groups of similar sites, use the **hub navigation.**
- **Local navigation** for a single site

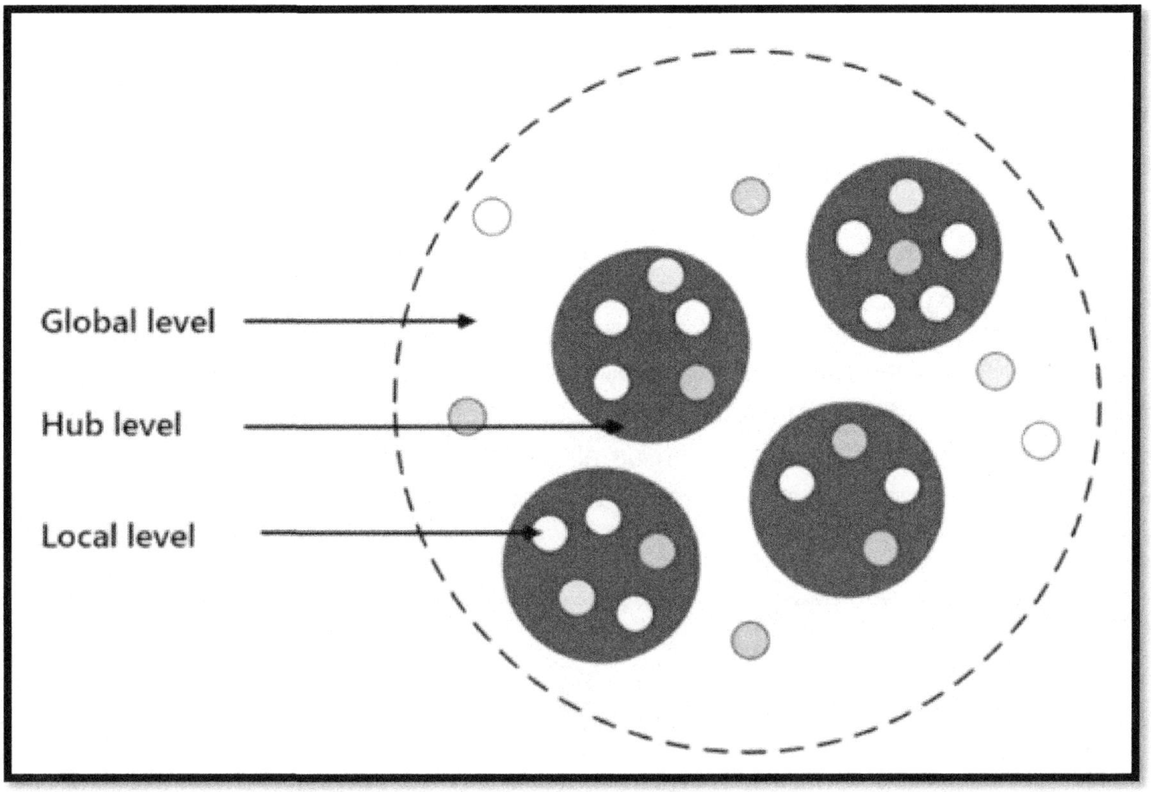

GLOBAL NAVIGATION

Many intranets include top-level access that is consistent across all sites. With global navigation, you can create a visual narrative for the navigation of your intranet that connects all the sites, data, and resources that users need to complete their tasks. The following terms are often used to describe these concepts, while every business has its own set of guidelines for what should be in-cluded in global navigation:

- "Home
- About Us
- News
- Working Here/Work Resources/Administrative Services/Administration
- Operations/ Operations Services
- Pay & Benefits
- Life& Career
- Locations
- Policies & Procedures/Tools & Resources/Safety & Security"

Facilitating information browsing is the goal of global navigation. Global navigation links often point to a large menu, sub-links, or primary category navigation pages in order to maximize the available space. This provides users with sufficient information to lo-cate the required material.

Since the context for global travel needs to be wide, it is challenging to create labels that are both comprehensive and helpful. If you wish to utilize global navigation, you should test your recommended navigation to make sure users like it.

You are able to browse the whole website using the SharePoint app bar on your home page.

You need a home page in order to make your website accessible to people worldwide. On the left, global access is available for each website and page.

HUB NAVIGATION

SharePoint hubs facilitate the grouping of websites connected by concept, project, division, department, or location. Hubs facilitate the discovery of news and other activity on connected websites. Additionally, you can check across all of the linked sites and utilize the same layout, branding, and site structure. One of the most crucial tasks when organizing a hub is organizing the hub navigation.

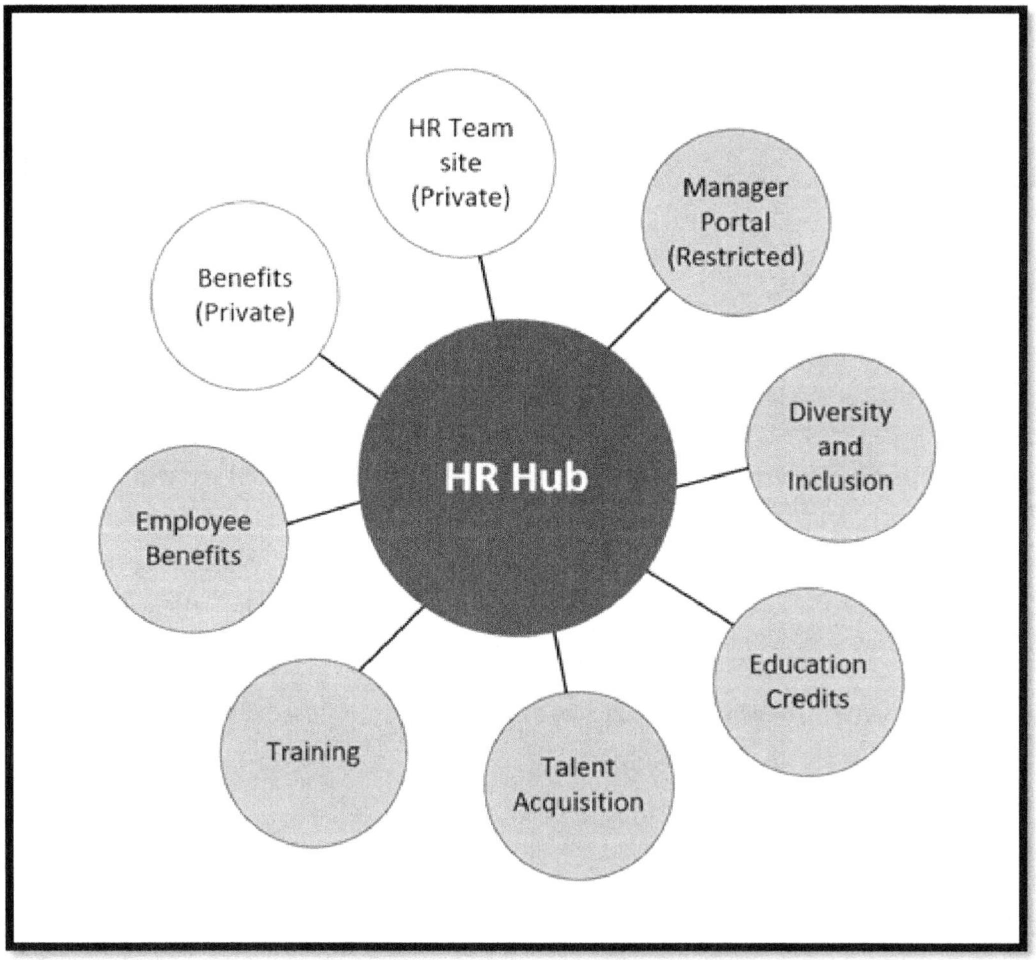

The hub navigation appears on each site just above the local navigation and under the suite bar. Hub routing is configured on the website which referred to as the hub. All the websites that are connected to it share it, and it is established by the hub owner.

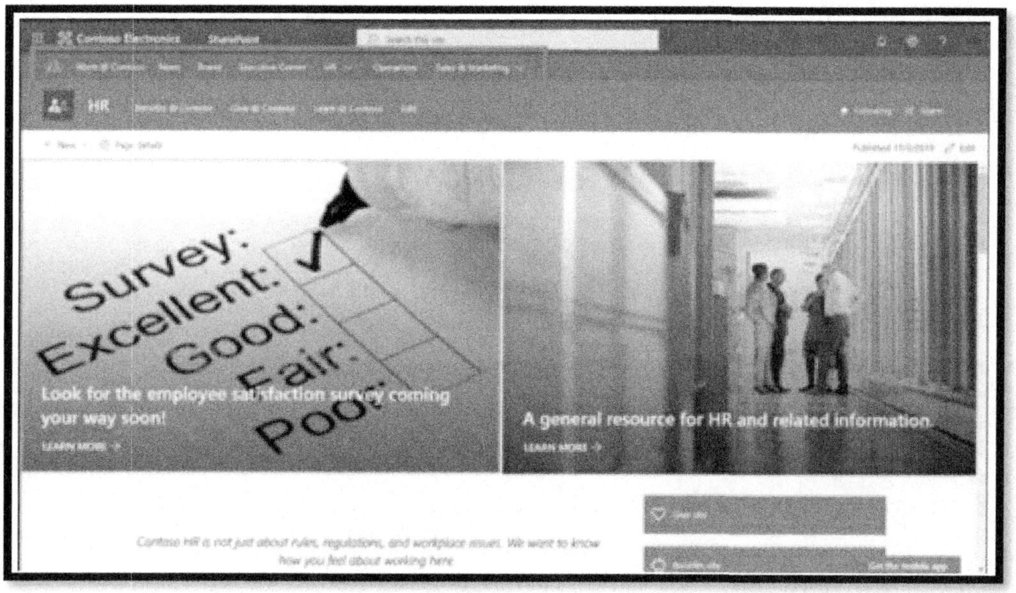

Every site can only be a part of one hub at a time. Nonetheless, as part of your navigation experience, you can join hubs together utilizing linked hubs and navigation links.

LOCAL NAVIGATION

The "**quick launch**" section on the left side of team sites is where you'll find this menu. Users can see the same navigation on every page of your website; this is known as "**local navigation**." The local menu bar appears at the top of contact websites.

Your website has local access on every page. If users can navigate between pages and information on several sites, they will remain on one site longer. Consider how users may wish to browse your content locally in order to facilitate their exploration.

The following are a few instances of local navigation links that you could see on a travel website. These links can be helpful to users who are looking at the site to plan their trip (before, during, and after) or to find out "What am I allowed to do?"

- **"Travel guidelines**
  - Air
  - Car
  - Ground Transportation
  - Hotel
  - Train
- **Before you go**
  - Travel approval
  - Booking service
- **During your trip**

- Travel safety
- Itinerary changes

- **After you return**
  - Expense reporting
  - Trip reports"

THE TEAM SITE NAVIGATION

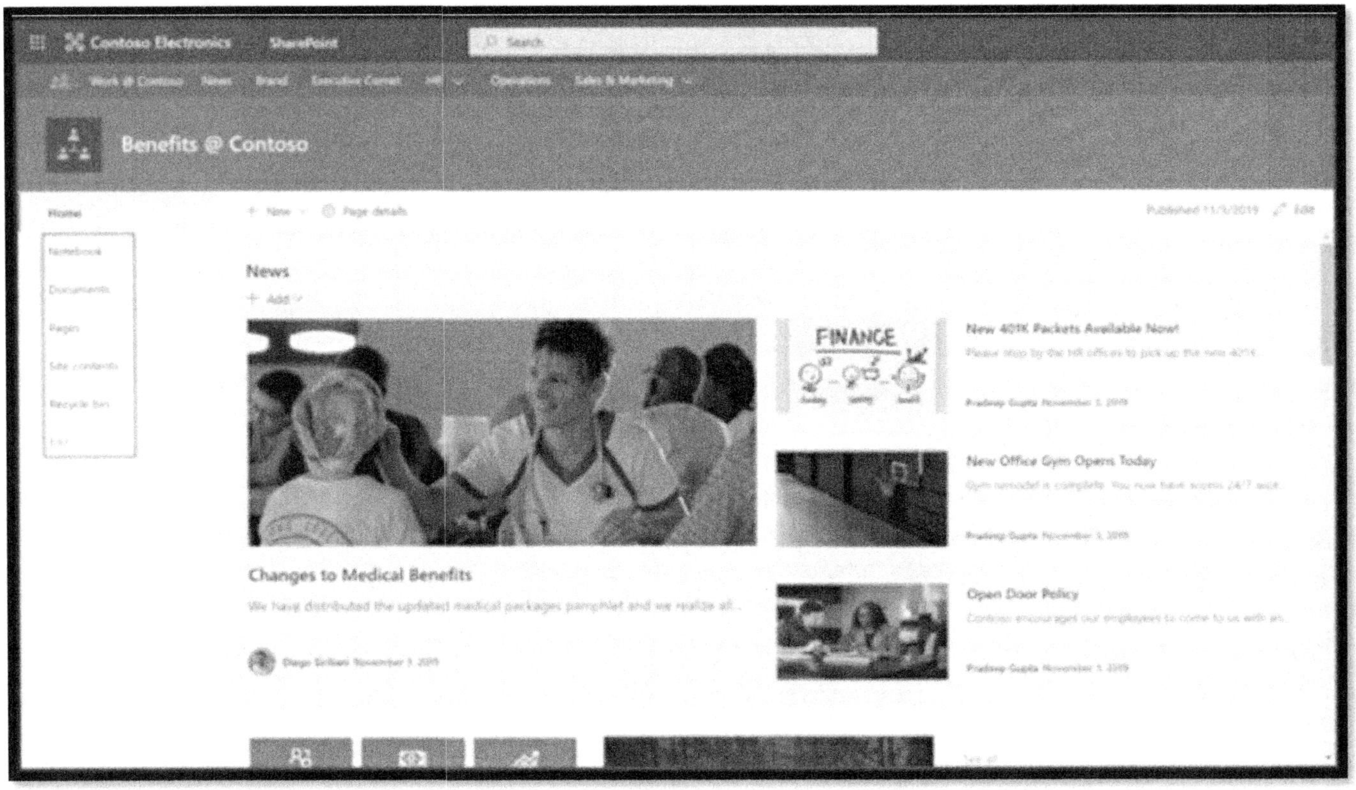

COMMUNICATION SITE NAVIGATION

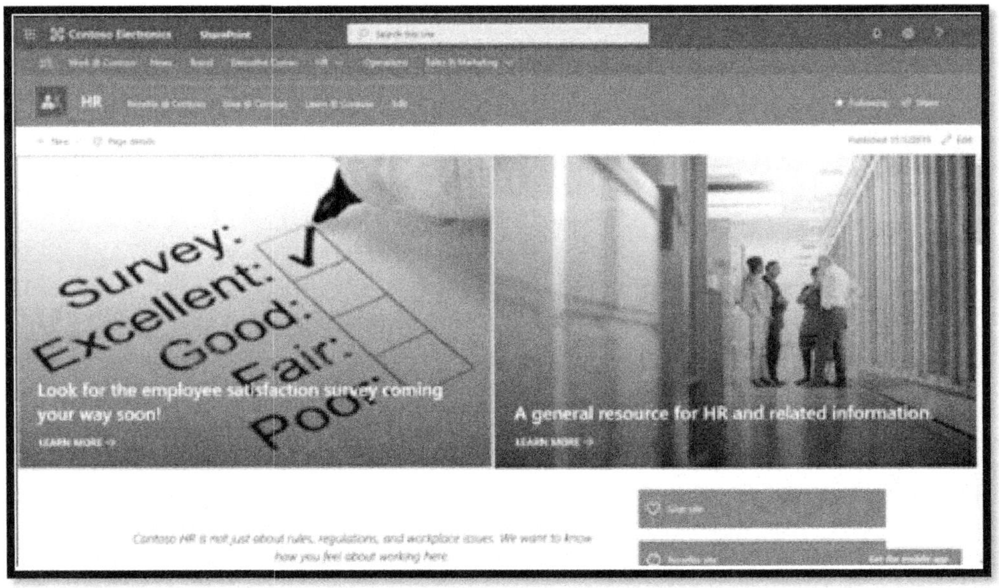

SITES

The communication and team sites that make up your intranet and portals provide you with additional access to the site's pages, lists, and libraries.

Current SharePoint team sites come with Microsoft 365 groups, which make information design simple to set up and maintain. As a membership service, Microsoft 365 groups make it simple to provide permissions to hubs and sites. They also provide additional functionality for Microsoft Teams and SharePoint team sites. With Microsoft 365 groups, you can provide a group of individuals access to collaboration tools such as Planner, OneNote, SharePoint team sites, and more. M365 groups can only be used on Share- Point team sites.

PAGES

On pages on team or communication sites, you can utilize web parts such as News, Highlighted material, or Sites, which are interac-tive web parts that can modify content from other sites and pages quickly. Every page on a website tells a story.

Your websites consist of three primary categories of pages:

- **The home page** contains an overview of the content of your website and information about what visitors can anticipate.
- Pages with alternatives or information summaries that assist users in choosing where to go next are known as **navigation pages.**
- On the **destination pages**, the reader's trip comes to an end. This is where you will post content for readers to read, print, or download. If your primary page is very detailed or you want to provide further information on a complex topic, you can create a subsidiary page.

You should consider how you present the content on each page since most users do not read the whole content or even scroll to the bottom. Ascertain that the most crucial information appears first on the page. Your viewers need this knowledge in order to com- prehend what you're trying to say.

As the page continues on, you can keep adding useful but optional content. This is analogous to starting your work from the beginning rather than the finish with your summary or conclusion. Use headings, bullet points, and section breaks to break up your pages and make them simpler to read.

NAVIGATIONAL ELEMENTS

These include navigation-assistance features like the bottom menu, waterfall menu, and enormous menu. Two instances of auxil-iary navigational components are buttons and inline links.

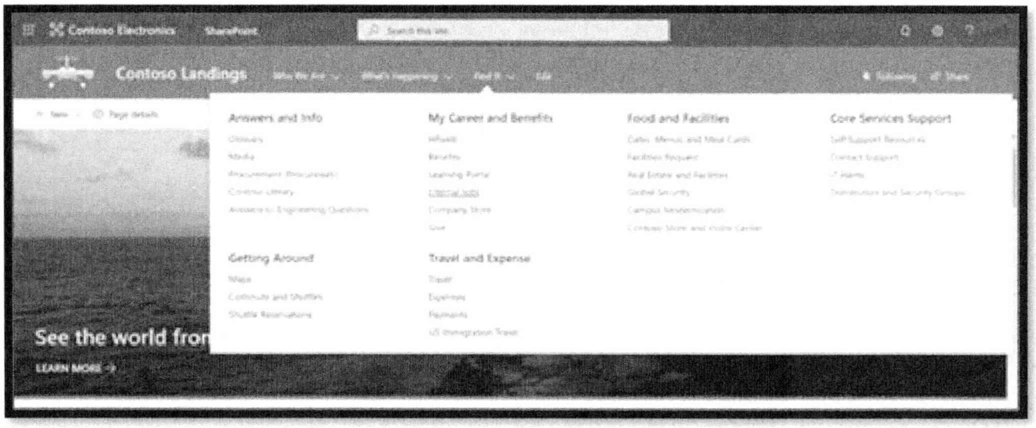

PERSONALIZATION ELEMENTS

1. The greatest content can reach the appropriate individuals with the use of **Audience Targeting.** Set audience targeting so that certain groups of people will see particular

content more prominently when using SharePoint web com- ponents, page libraries, and navigational links.
2. **Information Barriers** are restrictions that a compliance administrator can put up in Microsoft 365 to prevent users from communicating and cooperating with one another. This helps, for example, when one division is in control of information that shouldn't be shared with specific other divisions or when it's necessary to prevent one division from collaborating with any other division. Information barriers are often used in industries with stringent regula-tions, such as banking, law, and government.
3. **Multilingual Considerations:** If your organization employs individuals from a variety of cultural backgrounds, you may choose to provide multilingual content on your intranet sites. In the user interface, the user can choose the lan-guage in which to see the site navigation, title, and description. You can also provide pages and news items on com-munication sites that you translate into the user's preferred language.
4. For the site name, menu, and footer to appear in any of the numerous languages you provide, they must all be man-ually translated. Consider a communication website that you have accessible in Spanish and German in addition to English, where English is the default language. When you create a website, the name and description are automati-cally adjusted to the standard language. English in this instance. Even after the site has been created, you can alter its name and description. After that, you write the English text for the bottom and menu nodes.
5. A user whose first language is Spanish edits and manually converts the title, description, menu, and bottom content into Spanish after the website is first set up in English. A user selects German as their primary language and uses German in the same way. After it has been translated, the data will be seen by all users who speak those languages.

METADATA ARCHITECTURE

To organize pages and documents on your SharePoint site, you can utilize columns and content types, which are the two most crucial types of information. Metadata can be used to assist users in sorting and filtering content as well as in finding it in a list or library. Additionally, you should employ columns in your library of Site Pages so that you can link pages based on shared informa-tion by using highlighted content webparts.

A document's contents can also be arranged using folders, although they are fixed and difficult to modify. Folders can be useful in maintaining the efficiency and security of your document libraries. Never the less, more than two levels of nesting in a folder struc-ture complicate matters for users and should be avoided.

On a site, you can use more than one document library. One is provided at every site. To arrange the material inside the libraries and avoid creating several levels of folders within folders, you may choose to add topic-specific libraries and site columns to your in-tranet sites instead of utilizing the standard Documents library.

SEARCH EXPERIENCES

Most likely, you've already invested financial resources in information architecture. When users are unsure of where the content is located in your design, search can assist them in finding it. It also helps users find content they had not found before.

Tools such as symbols, notes, Q&A, floor layouts, and locations can be used in search to assist users in finding content and enhance search results.

CHAPTER 9: RECORDS MANAGEMENT AND ARCHIVING

RECORDS MANAGEMENT OVERVIEW

An object inside an organization that documents what the organization purchased or did and must be retained for a certain period of time is called a record, whet her it be a computer file or a paper copy. A business determines what sorts of information should be retained as records as it expands. We refer to this as records **management.**

- It determines whether data categories are appropriate for the records category.
- Determines how current documents that will be declared records should be handled and collected, as well as how they should be handled while in use.
- Decides how long each kind of record should be kept and how to do it in order to meet legal, business, or regulatory require-ments.
- Investigate and implement technological solutions and business practices to help ensure that the organization complies with its records management standards in an affordable and unobtrusive manner.
- Fulfills duties related to records, such as locating and keeping documents related to external events like litigation or discarding out-of-date records.

Identification of documents and other tangible or digital items in your organization that qualify as records is the responsibility of corporate compliance officials, records managers, and attorneys. These individuals can assist you in making sure that documents are retained for the appropriate length of time by meticulously arranging all of the business material for your firm. A well-designed records management system has many advantages, including enhanced organizational speed, legal protection, and regulatory compliance. This is so that it promotes the appropriate disposal of outdated materials that aren't records

The following components are included in a records management system:

- **A content analysis** that lists and arranges the content in the company that can be converted into records, as well as the con- tent's sources and the paths it will travel to reach the records management application.
- **A file plan** should be in place that lists where each sort of business record should be stored, the regulations that apply, how long it should be retained, how to dispose of it, and who is responsible for managing it.
- **A document outlining compliance standards** that describes the rules that the organization's IT systems must follow in order to ensure compliance and the steps taken to ensure the participation of enterprise team members.
- **Away to gather files and records that are no longer being used** from all record sources, including file servers, email systems, and collaboration servers.
- **A way to check records** while they are being used.
- **A way to keep track of the metadata** and review records logs.
- **Away to keep records** (delay their destruction) until certain events, such as litigation, take place.

- **A way to monitor and report on how records** are being handled is to ensure that employees are abiding by the guidelines and standards when they submit, access, and manage records.

Businesses can establish collaborative systems and procedures for maintaining records by using SharePoint's functionalities.

OVERVIEW OF RECORDS MANAGEMENT PLANNING

This section discusses the preparation steps you should take to ensure that the SharePoint-based records management system you put up will support your organization's records management objectives. An outline of the records management planning procedure is provided below:

1. **Identify Records Management Roles:** The organization's data must be organized and the records management process must be overseen by designated personnel, such as compliance officers and records managers, in order for records management to function effectively.

- IT personnel to put up the instruments necessary for effective record-keeping.
- Content managers are responsible for ensuring that their teams adhere to the company's record-keeping policies and for knowing where the records are maintained.

2. **Analyze organizational content:** Content managers and records managers examine how documents are utilized inside the organization to determine which ones can be converted into records before creating a file plan.
3. **Make a file plan:** After examining the content of your group and determining how long to retain items, complete the remaining sections of the file plan. File plans vary from firm to company, but generally speaking, they list the kinds of items the company views as records, where they are stored, how long they are maintained, who is responsible for them, and what broader group of records they are a part of.
4. **Develop retention schedules**: Determine when each sort of record is no longer active (being used), how long it should be maintained after that, and how to properly dispose of it when it is no longer needed.
5. **Evaluate and enhance document management procedures:** Additionally, ensure that all regulations are being fol-lowed in locations where documents are stored. To ensure that the appropriate reports are stored with the records, for example, ensure that the information is examined accurately.
6. **Design the records management solution**: Decide whether to treat the records as they are, create a backup copy, or combine the two. strategy the record collection using your file strategy, or find ways to store records on existing sites. Configure libraries, rules, content kinds, and, if necessary, data directing the system to transmit a document.
7. **Plan how content turns into records:** If you use SharePoint for both active document management and document management, you can automate the process of moving content to a records library. If you use an external document management system or SharePoint, you can design and create connections that designate a document as a record but do not move it, or that transfer material from those systems to the records folder. You also design how users will be trained to create and manipulate records.
8. **Plan email integration:** Select whether SharePoint or the email tool itself will be used to manage your email records.

9. **Plan Compliance for Social Content:** Det erm in e how information from blogs, wikis, and other social media plat- forms will be converted into records if your firm utilizes them.
10. **Plan Compliance Reporting and Documentation:** To ensure that your company is adhering to records management regulations and to disseminate information about these regulations, you should put your records management policies and procedures in writing. For instance, you may have to provide these records management guidelines, im-plementation plans, and performance metrics in the event that your business is sued over documents.

OVERVIEW OF SHAREPOINT RECORD CENTERS

We can refer to the procedure that the record center site collection handles as "record archiving" since it involves automatically keeping old documents in one location.

You can utilize it in a variety of ways. One method is to use it as a central repository for documents. For example, the well-known SharePoint list view threshold issue may occur if the active document library becomes too full after a few days due to a large number of documents.

To avoid this, the old documents must be transferred to a new site- basically, a document center. The document will be transferred to the record center site if the requirements outlined in the content type IRM (Information Right Management) policy are fulfilled. I will address this in greater detail in the next section.

If you want to handle all of your documents in one location, you may also utilize it. You may wish to submit all of your documents to one location and have them automatically sent to the relevant websites, for instance, if you have documents pertaining to law, finance, sales, purchase orders, and so on. By setting up content organizer rules on the record center website, you can do this.

However, take note:

- Documents cannot be removed from the record library once they are locked. There cord center takes care of this automati-cally.
- Even better, we can create a record on the team site by documenting it, but first, we must utilize Power Automate or build up a routine.
- Since it's the final step of a document's lifespan, the record stage is locked.

We can now clearly define a SharePoint Online record center and see the need for one. Next, we will discuss how to configure the system for archiving.

HOW TO SET UP THE RECORD CENTER ARCHIVING MECHANISM IN SHAREPOINT ONLINE?

The record center in SharePoint Online can be set up in three steps:

- Assemble a collection of record center sites
- Establish the record center connection in Microsoft 36S Record Center;
- Create and configure the record center site collection's content organizer rule.

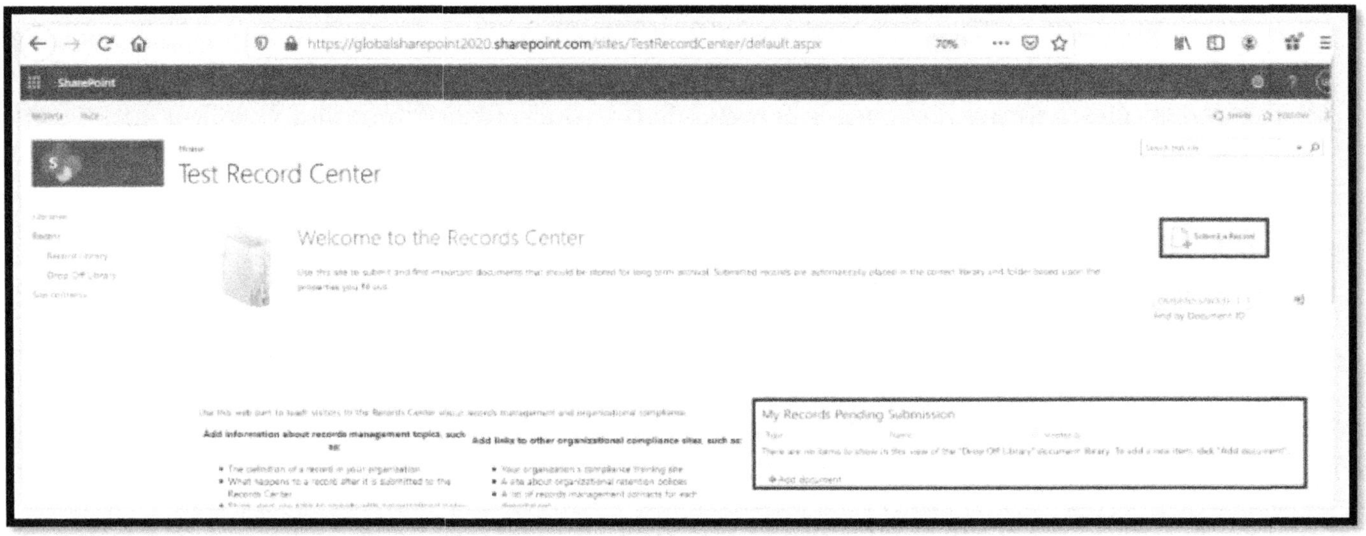

- Go to the **settings page** of the site
- Navigate to the **Site Administration area** and choose "**Content Organizer settings**".
- The screen where we can adjust the Content organizer settings will then appear.

You need to take note of this webservice URL:

https://globalsharepoint2020.sharepoint.com/sites/TestRecordCenter/_vti_bin/OfficialFile.asmx
We will want this webservice URL when we configure the connection to the record center inside the Microsoft 36S admin center; please keep this in mind.

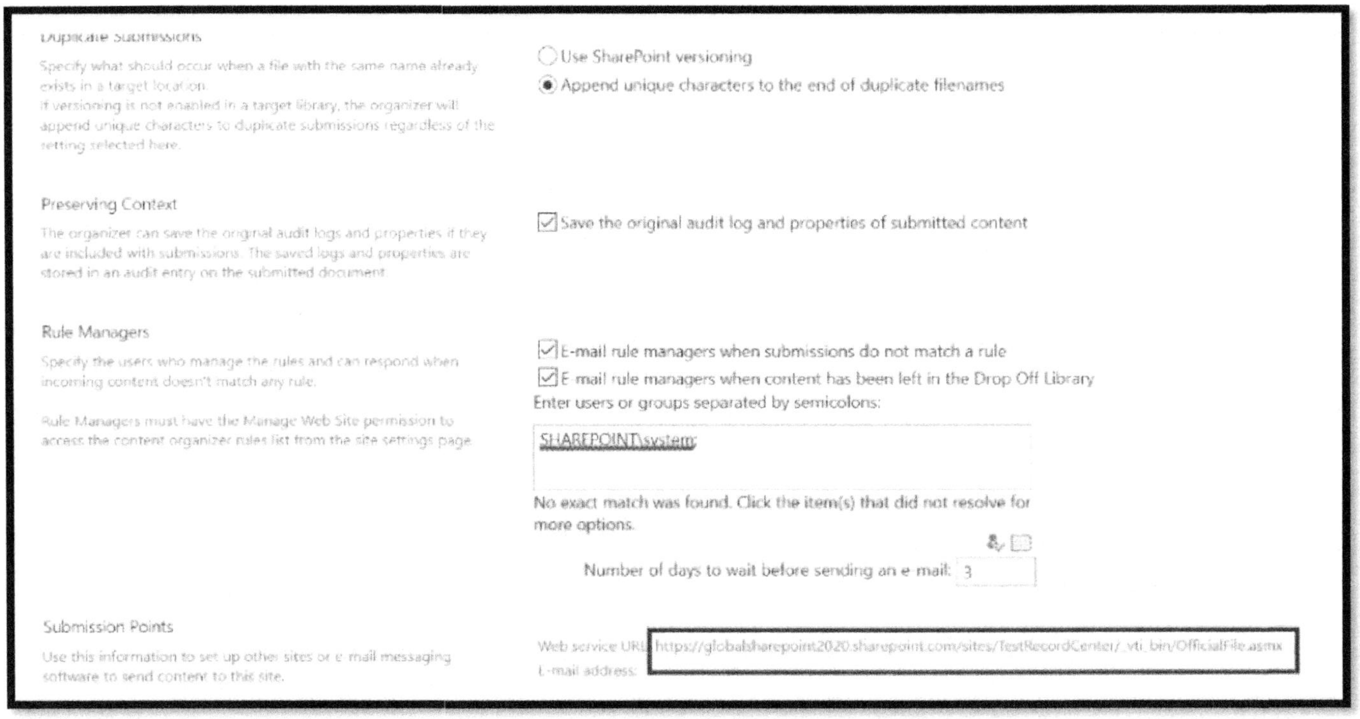

CHAPTER 10: CUSTOMIZING YOUR SHAREPOINT SITE

SITE CUSTOMIZATION BASICS

- Modify the main menu, picture, title, and design of your website. You can utilize the Change the Appearance option in the site settings to choose from a variety of designs, layouts, and colors. You can also add your brand and modify the links on the menu of your website.

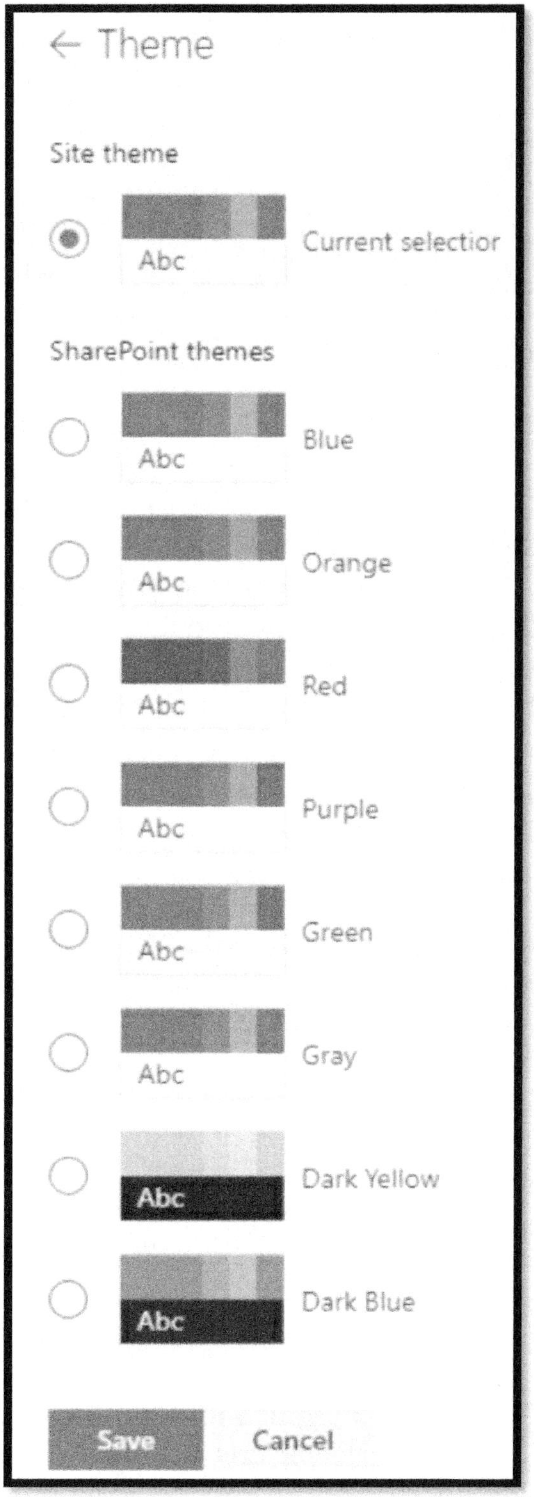

- Make your website seem template-like. Certain site themes in SharePoint include pre-filled and functional pages, news post templates, page templates, and web elements. You can modify these templates to suit your requirements. For example, you can use the Event template to inform people about a forthcoming event or the Human Resources template to inform employees about benefits, career opportunities, compensation, and corporate policies.
- Web components let you add dynamic and helpful content to your site's pages. Web components are reusable elements that display information or content from several sources. With web components, you can customize your site pages with text, images, videos, charts, maps, forms, and more. You can also modify the appearance and functionality of web components to suit your requirements.

PUTTING IN QUICK LINKS

One fantastic feature of SharePoint is its quick connections. To access frequently accessed sites or critical information, just click on them. Adding fast connections to SharePoint is simple. By creating easy connections to frequently used tools, it saves time. Files, team websites, and other websites can all be accessed by them.

- Navigate to the desired page first for the link to appear. To make modifications, choose "**Edit**." Locate a section of the page, such as the web component or content area.
- Proceed by selecting"+ **Adda new web part**." This displays a list of site components. Click on the "**Quick Links**" section of the website.
- To make modifications, click the pencil button located in the Quick Links web part's upper right corner. It seems like a screen that pops out. Links can be added and grouped.
- To add a link, choose the "+ **Add Link**" button. You can enter the URL and title of the link in a box that will appear. If you would want a new tab to open, you can choose one.
- Repeat these steps for each link. Click someplace else to save when you're finished. It will be possible to access your fast links now that you have them.

WHAT ARE SHAREPOINT WEB PARTS?

Simply put, webparts are elements on a page that display data. It's similar to piecing together a website page using jigsaw pieces. These web components are little programs that, depending on the web component, save and display different types of data.

Web components for SharePoint are preconfigured. However, you can utilize third-party webparts- which are available in Micro- soft 365-on your website. You can add pre-made web components to your site pages that display a variety of functions and types of information. Unboxed computer components include such like;

- **News web part:** You can display news stories from your website or other websites in a variety of formats and styles with this web component. The news can also be sorted by topic, date, or source.
- **Event webpart:** Future events from your site or other sites can be shown in a schedule or list view with the aid of the Events web component. Additionally, you can link the events to Outlook or other calendars.

- **Highlighted content web part (HCWP):** Th is web component allows you to dynamically display material from your website or other websites depending on criteria such as content type, information, or keywords. The appearance and functional-ity of the web section can both be altered.

ADD APPS FOR SHAREPOINT-TO-SHAREPOINT SITES

Owners of websites can add SharePoint applications from the following sources:

- From the list of pre-installed apps (which includes pre-purchased apps as well as fundamental apps like standard libraries and lists).
- Via the App Store.
- From the store for SharePoint.

Remember that an application cannot be launched by someone signed in as a system account.

When you add the application to SharePoint, it requests the necessary permissions to function (such as access to Search or the abil-ity to create lists). If you don't have certain permissions, this app will not function. Ask your supervisor for the necessary permis-sions, or have someone else install the app on their behalf. The procedures to add applications from these locations are as follows.

- Make sure the user account doing this isa member of the site Owners group before adding an app from the list of applications that can be used on the site.
- On your homepage, click the button that says **"Add lists, libraries, and other apps"** next to "Get started with your site."

If it's not on the front page, you can begin managing your site. Click the Settings button and choose View Site Contents to do this. Finally, choose Add an App from the Site Contents tab.

- Choose the app to add to the list of **"Your Apps"** by clicking on it.
- If it's a custom component, trust the application and adhere to the instructions. Give the app a name if it's a SharePoint component.

You can now find the SharePoint app in the **Apps section** of your Site Contents list.

ADDING AN APP FROM THE APP STORE

- First, confirm that the account being used for this is a member of the site owners group.
- On your homepage, click the button that says "**Add lists, libraries, and other apps"** next to **"Ge t started with your site."**

If it's not on the front page, you can begin managing your site. Click the Settings button and choose View Site Contents to do this. Finally, choose Add an App from the Site Con t ents tab.

- Select "**From Name**" by clicking on it

Name is the name of your company's App Catalog. "From Contoso" is one such instance.

Note: Applications designated as "**Featured**" in the App Catalog will also appear in the main app list.

- Select an app to include.
- Select "**Allow Access**" from the "**Grant Permission to an App"** dialog box if you think the app is legitimate.

You can now find the SharePoint app in the Apps section of your Site Contents list. To include a SharePoint Store for application;

- First, confirm that the account being used for this isa member of the site owners group.
- On your homepage, click the button that says**" Add lists, libraries, and other apps**" next to "Get started with your site."

If it's not on the front page, you can begin managing your site. Click the Settings button and choose View Site Contents to do this. Finally, choose Add an App from the Site Contents tab.

- Select the SharePoint Store
- To find the desired software, browse the SharePoint Store.
- Select an app to include.
- Select **"Read More**" and then "**Buy It."**
- Follow the instructions to participate and, if necessary, purchase the app.
- Click **Allow Access** in the **Grant Permission to an app** dialog box, if you think the program is legitimate. You can now find the SharePoint app in the Apps section of your Site Contents list.

CHAPTER 11: WORKING WITH DOCUMENT LIBRARIES

UNDERSTANDING DOCUMENT LIBRARIES

A document library in SharePoint is a location to store and organize files. If you have an internet connection, you can use it as a virtual file cabinet anytime you want. SharePoint's document library allows you to create, publish, edit, and share files with your team straight instantly. You can collaborate on projects, see multiple revisions, and manage all of your documents in one place.

Document Libraries save you time and effort while also allowing you to use advanced search capabilities and sort documents. Set- ting permissions, categorizing documents, and having version control are just a few of the fundamental capabilities of SharePoint Document Library that make it a valuable tool for document management. Document Libraries allow us to ensure that all of our team members can view and utilize our materials, which increases cooperation and efficiency.

Modern SharePoint Document Libraries have sophisticated capabilities that enhance collaboration and efficiency, such as process automation, co-authoring, and OneDrive synchronization.

PLAN YOUR DOCUMENT LIBRARY IN SHAREPOINT

In SharePoint, developing a well-structured Document Library entail determining what the firm requires, creating the appropriate structure, and updating information and views to make documents easier to discover and organize.

To create an expandable SharePoint Document Library framework, consider the following steps: planning the information architecture, establishing a hierarchical structure, determining the type of library, using metadata for document discover ability and cat-egorization, creating document sets, implementing version control, and considering security and permissions.

CREATE AND MANAGE SHAREPOINT DOCUMENT LIBRARIES

Automatic Creation of Default Document Library

When you create a new SharePoint site, it includes a document library named "Documents" that integrates seamlessly with the site's homepage. This feature is produced automatically and may serve as a beginning point for files and documents. It can be en-hanced by adding new document libraries to assist organize and manage a broader variety of files, depending on the demands of the collaborative team.

HOW TO CREAT E A DOCUMENT LIBRARY IN SHA REPOINT?

Creating a new document library in SharePoint is a straightforward procedure.

Here's how you can do it:

1. Establish the library of documents at the desired site.
2. Click **"New"** in the menu and choose **"Document Library"** from the list of available applications.
3. Create your library by clicking **"Create"** and naming it. Your document library will then be created.

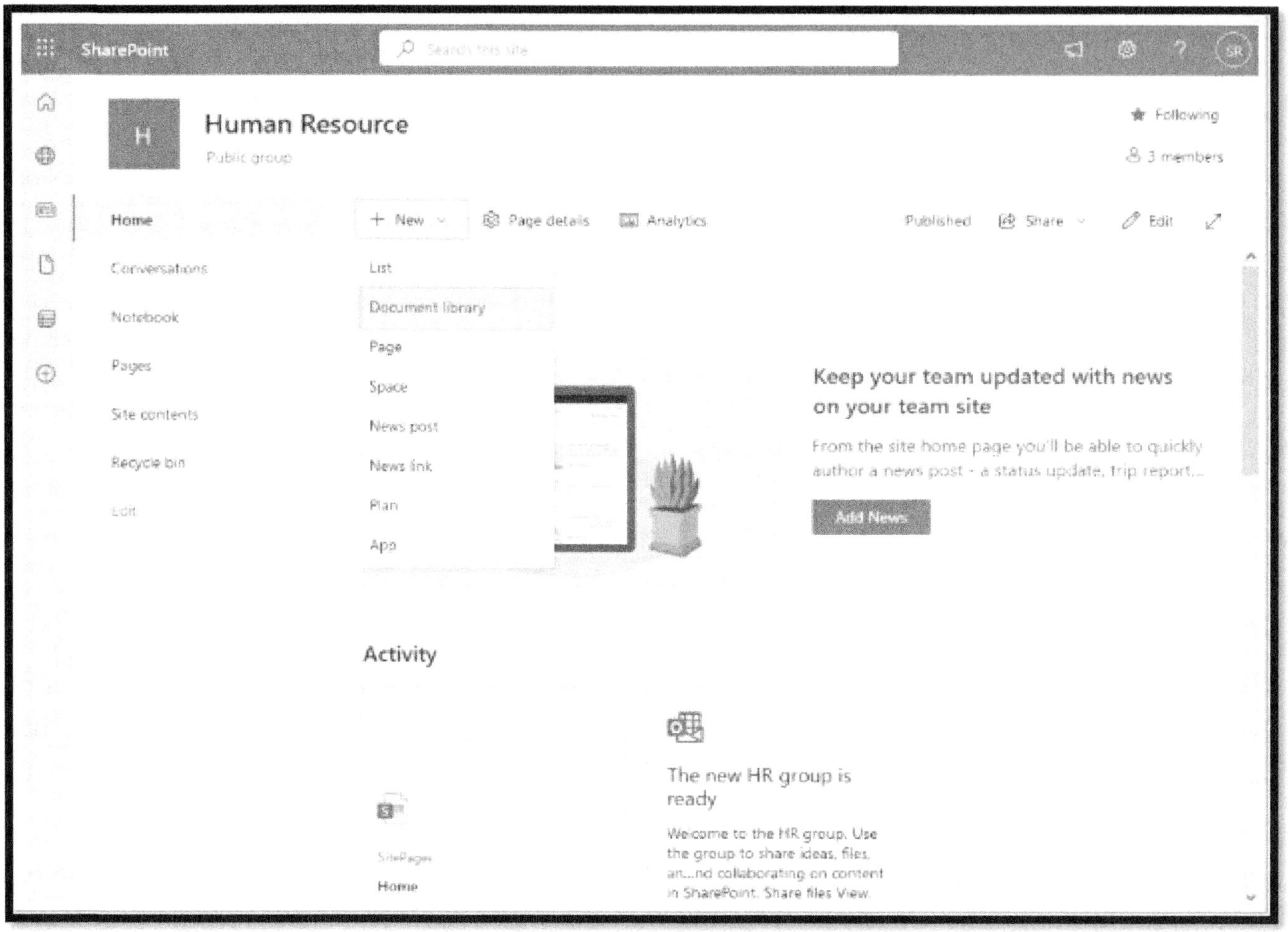

After you 've created your document library, you may customize it by adding columns, defining privileges, and adding themes. SharePoint has more than simply document libraries. You may keep files in the Picture Library, Form Library, Wiki page Library, Style Library, and so on.

GIVE YOUR LIBRARY A NAME AND SOME DETAILS

It is critical to give your library a name that appropriately defines what it is for. This will assist everyone on the team in recognizing and locating the library on the SharePoint site collection.

To provide more information about the library, add the following sentence to the library settings:

- Find the library you want to provide a description for.
- To alter library settings, use the gear symbol in the Settings menu.
- Add a name and description to the library in the Settings window.
- Click **Save.**

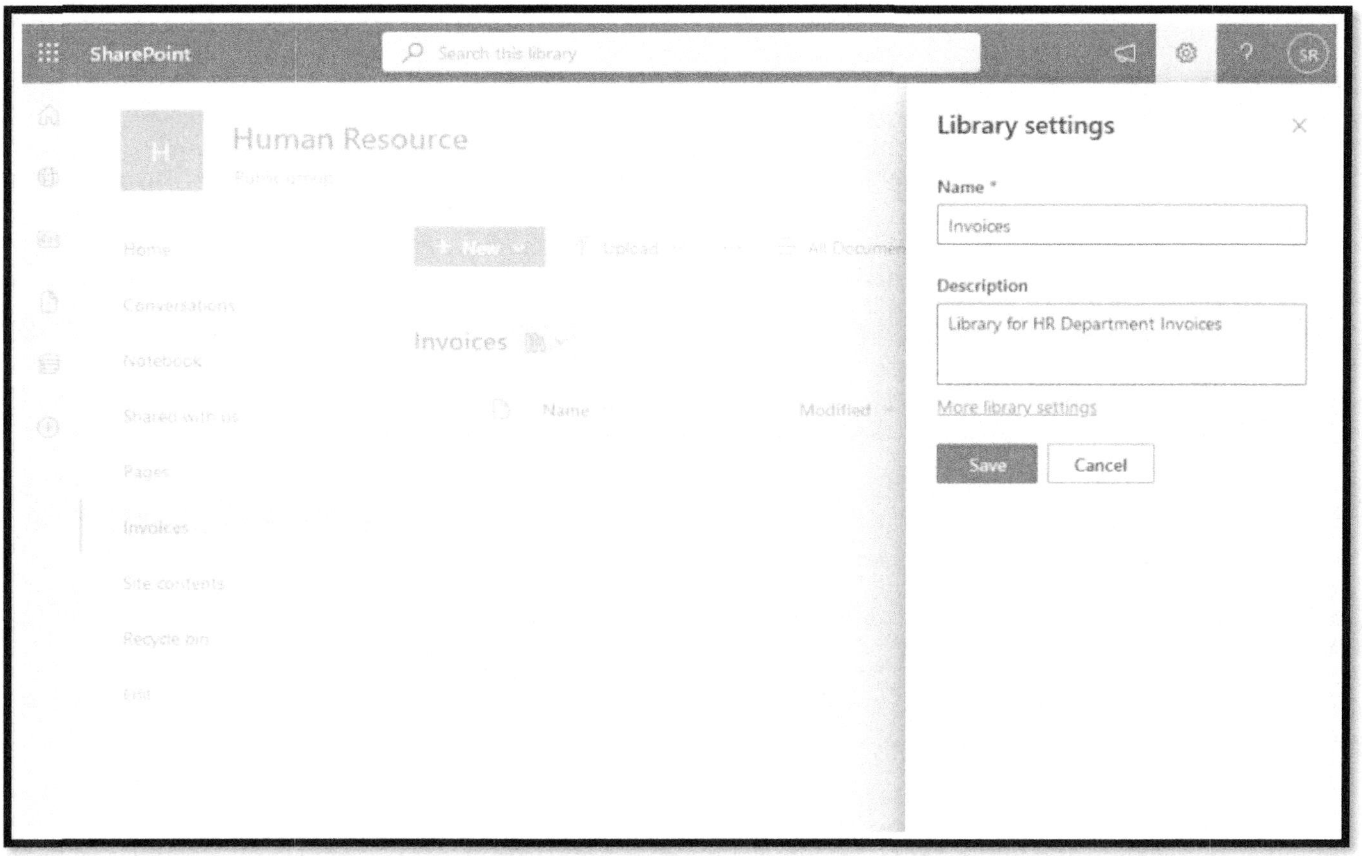

MANAGING DOCUMENT LIBRARY SETTINGS

To better organize your library and its files, you can assign each file's characteristics and metadata.

1. Identify the library that has the features you would like to change.
2. To make changes, go to **"Settings"> "Library setting s" > "More Library settings**."
3. Configure parameters on the document library settings page, including name, description, and any other informa-tion.
4. To apply changes, click "**Save**."

Following these instructions will allow you to successfully create and manage a SharePoint Document Library. This will provide your team with a well-organized and easily accessible place to keep their files.

EXPORTING THE SHAREPOINT DOCUMENT LIBRARY

It is useful to be able to share the document library from SharePoint while managing the library. This approach allows users to download a copy of the document library and save it for future use.

The steps below will help you export:

1. Navigate to your document library and choose the "**Library**" option.
2. To launch Windows Explorer and open the library, choose "**Open with Explorer**."
3. Select the folders and files you want to send overseas.

4. Move the files to the desired location.

You can also choose files and folders from the document library and click the "**Download**" option in the menu to download them.

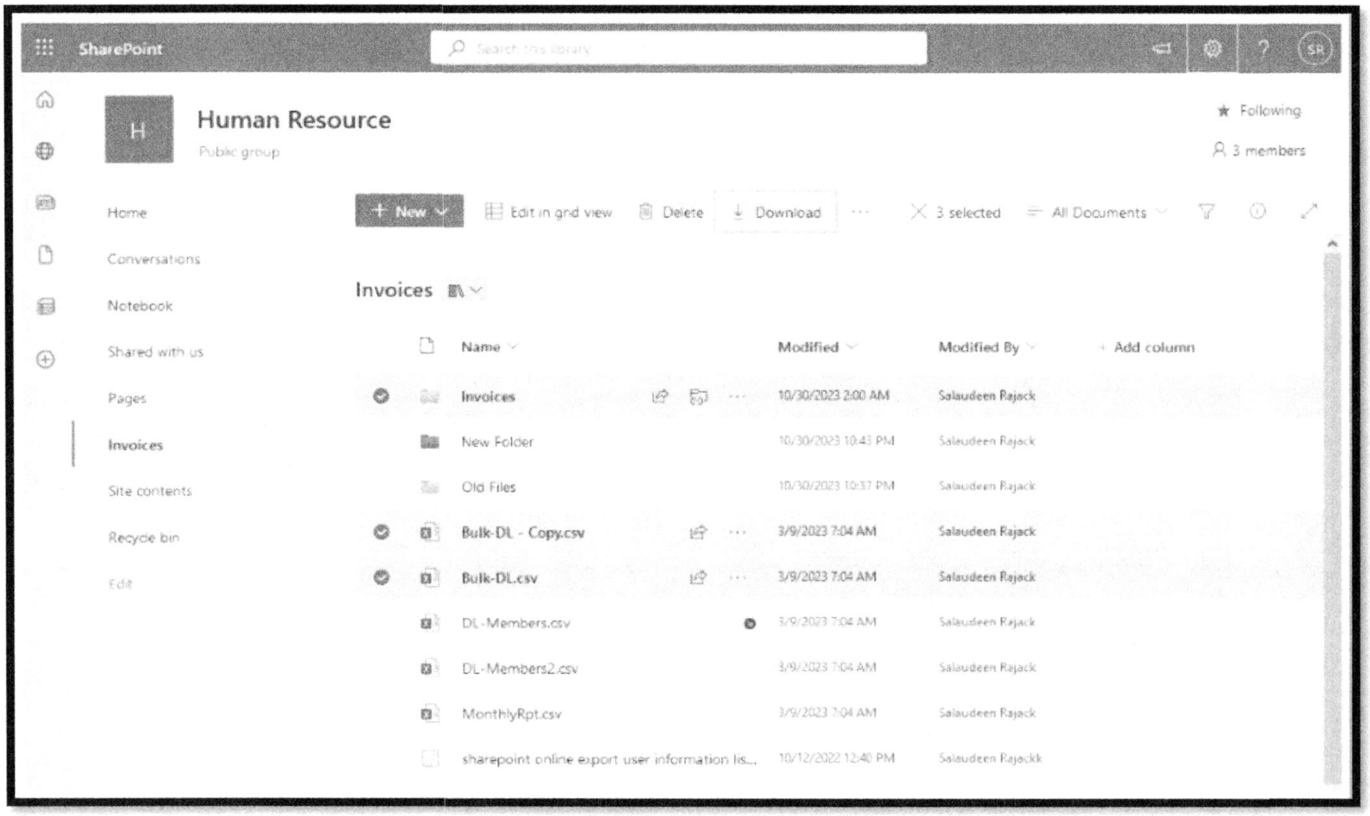

Users can improve the effectiveness of SharePoint's document library system by adopting these advanced capabilities, resulting in more effective and seamless communication.

To share the information from your SharePoint document library, take these steps:

1. To copy, go to the **SharePoint document library**.
2. Select the "**Export to Excel**" option under the Library menu.
3. Launch the created Excel file and save it.

REMOVING THE DOCUMENT LIBRARY IN SHAREPOINT

To modify the name of your SharePoint document library or remove it, take these steps:

1. Navigate to your document library and choose the "**Library**" option.
2. To remove this document library, choose "**Library Settings**" and then "**Title, description, and navigation.**"
3. To remove the document library, follow the instructions on the screen.

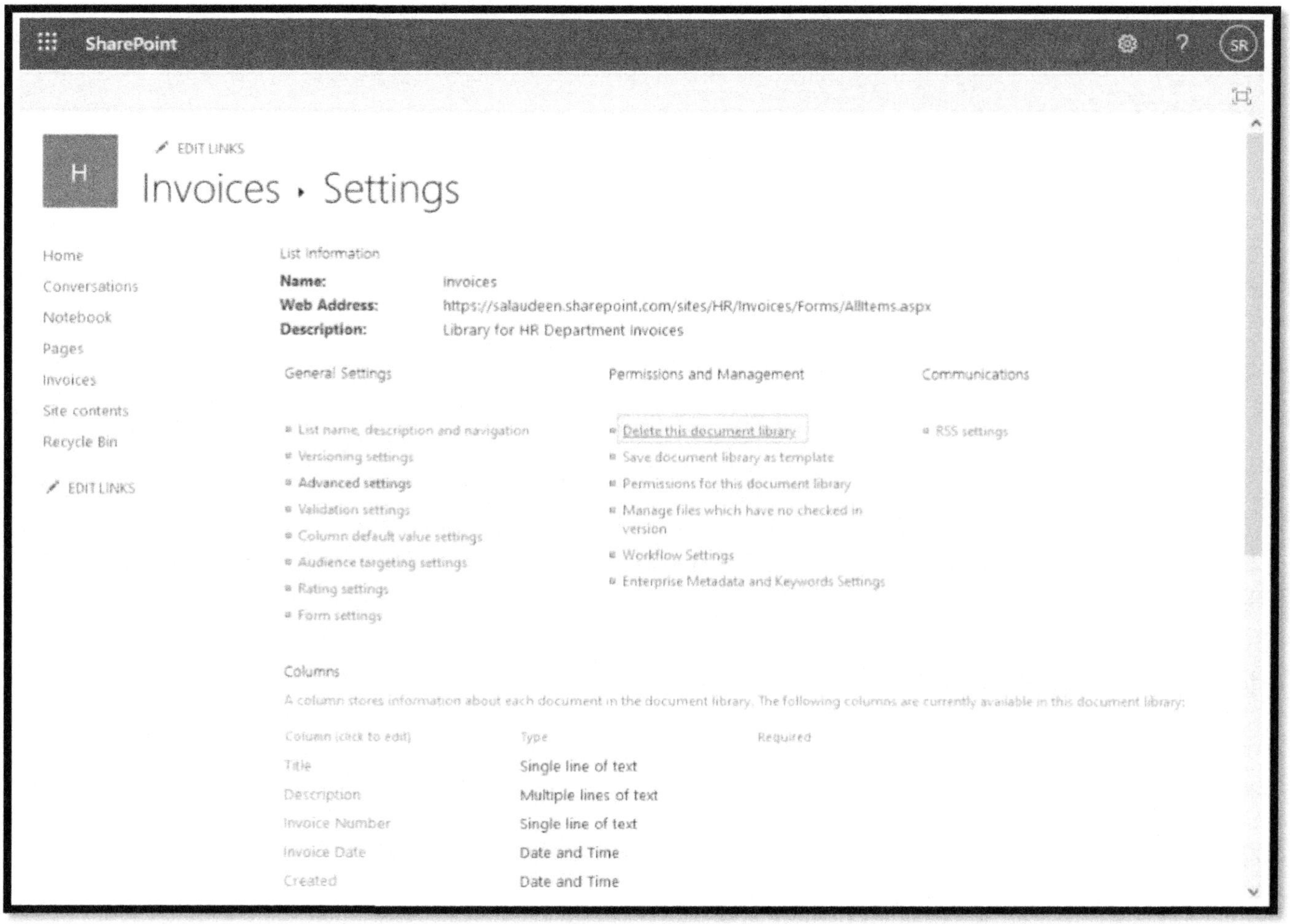

UPLOADING AND MANAGING DOCUMENTS

Uploading Files to SharePoint

Uploading files to SharePoint is a straightforward procedure that allows you to easily store and share your files. Share Point allows you to easily share and organize your files, whether you're working on a Word document, an Excel table, or a PowerPoint presentation.

Here's how to add a file to SharePoint:

1. Find the SharePoint site where you wish to add the file.
2. Locate the "**Upload**" link or button. (**Note: It normally appears toward the top of the page**).
3. To open the file upload window, choose the "**Upload**" button or link.
4. In the window that appears, click "**Browse**" to locate the file on your computer that you want to share.
5. Click **"Open"** after selecting the file.
6. Again, within the share box, you can provide additional information about the file, such as a title or description.
7. Once you've filled out all of the relevant information, click the "**Upload**" button to start the upload process.

8. The upload time may vary based on the size of the file and the speed of your internet connection. You'll notice a progress meter that indicates how the upload is proceeding.
9. When the upload is complete, you'll notice a message or alert indicating that the file was correctly submitted.

View and Edit SharePoint Documents

After you've uploaded your documents to SharePoint, you can quickly view and edit them in your web browser. This eliminates the need to download, modify, and re-share files.

These procedures will allow you to see and modify a SharePoint document:

1. Access the document on the SharePoint site.
2. Locate the file you want to view or update.
3. Click on the file's name or picture to open it in the browser.
4. The document will open in the software associated with the file type by default. For example, Word files will open in Word Online, while Excel files will open in Excel Online.
5. After the file has been opened, changes can be made to the text, style, or layout, exactly as in a desktop application.
6. SharePoint automatically saves changes as you work, eliminating the need to manually save the text.
7. SharePoint identifies and highlights real-time modifications made by several users on the same document.

CHAPTER 12: ADVANCED SEARCH AND CONTENT DISCOVERY

OVERVIEW OF SEARCH IN SHAREPOINT

If you are in charge of search inside your company, you should educate yourself on how to tailor the search experience to your orga-nization's requirements and make the search even more useful to your users.

SharePoint in Microsoft 365 offers both conventional and modern search experiences. The contemporary search experience in-cludes access to Microsoft Search in SharePoint. The most obvious difference is that the Microsoft Search box is shown in the header bar, which is positioned at the very top of SharePoint. Another distinguishing feature is that Microsoft Search is a personal search.

Even when searching for the same terms, the results obtained by one user varied significantly from those obtained by other users. Before entering the search field, users are given results based on their previous behavior and current trending content in Microsoft 365.

These results are updated as the user writes. Since you are the administrator, the search results are easy to explore and need no work on your end. When it comes to discovering search results, both search experiences utilize the same index. Beyond what is available with Microsoft Search in SharePoint, the traditional search experience may be tweaked and adjusted to your specific re-quirements. Some conventional search settings may have an impact on both experiences; it is critical to understand how to avoid this from happening with Microsoft Search.

HOW SEARCH WORKS

This high-level explanation of how search works will help you understand where and how to change the search in SharePoint. Site columns are used to store special information about each document in lists and libraries.

1. The search index is updated with site columns and values when the crawler completes work on lists and libraries.
2. Site columns are associated with managed properties in the search index.
3. When a user enters a query in the search box, it is shared with the search index.
4. The search engine finds relevant results and redirects users to a website displaying them.

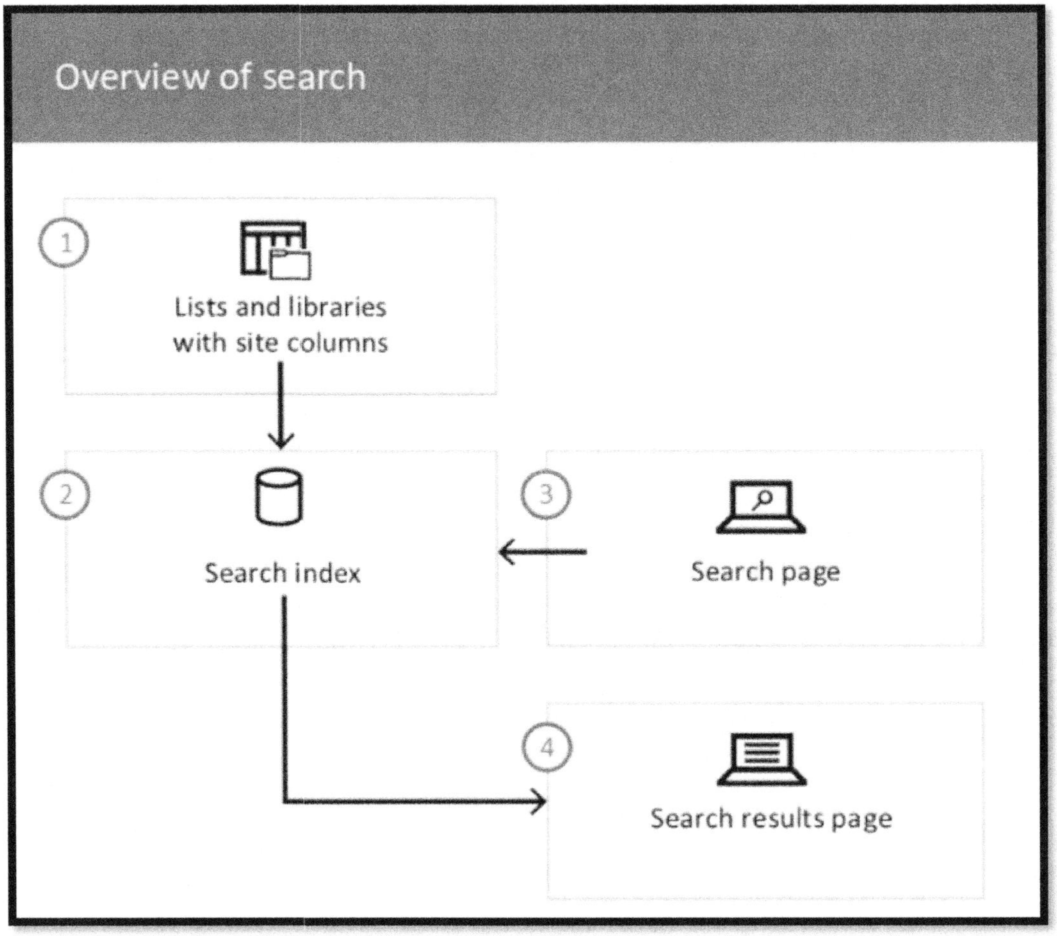

CREATE A CUSTOM SEARCH RESULTS PAGE IN SHAREPOINT ONLINE

Creating a custom search results page for a site is one way to tailor the search experience for SharePoint users. When you use a custom page instead of the default page that appears in Microsoft Search results, you can use the page that you created. When you use a page that is tailored to your visitors' requirements, you give them greater influence over how the search results look.

Using a custom results page, you may create a new page that can be used to modify the style and look of search results to meet your company's needs. You can use any of the built -in web parts, any open-source search web parts published by the SharePoint Patterns and Practices community, and any custom web parts created using SharePoint Framework.

SETTING UP A RESULTS PAGE

To set up a custom results page in SharePoint, follow the instructions below:

1. To implement a tailored results page on a website, go to the **Site Settings menu**, then **Site Collection Settings, then Search Settings.**
2. Remove the checkbox from the **"Use the same results page settings as my parent"** box in Search Settings, choose "**Send queries to a custom results page**, "and enter a value for the Results page URL field. You should then save your changes.

For example, **"https ://contoso.sharepoint.com/sites/search/SitePages/results.aspx"**

is a URL that should be entered here. This URL should be for the page you created to serve as your personalized results page.

Alternatively, you can change the value using the adjust-PnPSeacrhSettings SharePoint PnP PowerShell command instead of the Site Settings page.

Once set, the page displaying the results of your custom search will appear anytime you use the Microsoft Search box to perform a search. This box is positioned in the navigation bar at the top of the page and is used to input search terms from site pages or the website's homepage. You do not use it while searching inside a list, library, or on a website's content page. You may use the link to expand your search beyond the results of your search in lists and libraries to the page that shows your personalized results.

CHANGE THE LAYOUT OF YOUR CUSTOM RESULTS PAGE

HeaderlessSearch Results is a page layout that may be used to make the search results page seem more like the experience we get when using our default search results. This new layout may only be enabled on sites that are chosen to serve as the page for custom search results.

To define the page layout, use the Set-PnPPage PnP PowerShell command and the -LayoutType HeaderlessSearchResults argument.

ADVANCED SEARCH FEATURES AND SYNTAX

SharePoint's advanced search page is not the most obvious feature of the platform. When you use advanced search, there is no need to spell out search operators since it enables you to include logic in your search. You will discover that this Is really helpful in narrowing your results to be as appropriate as possible.

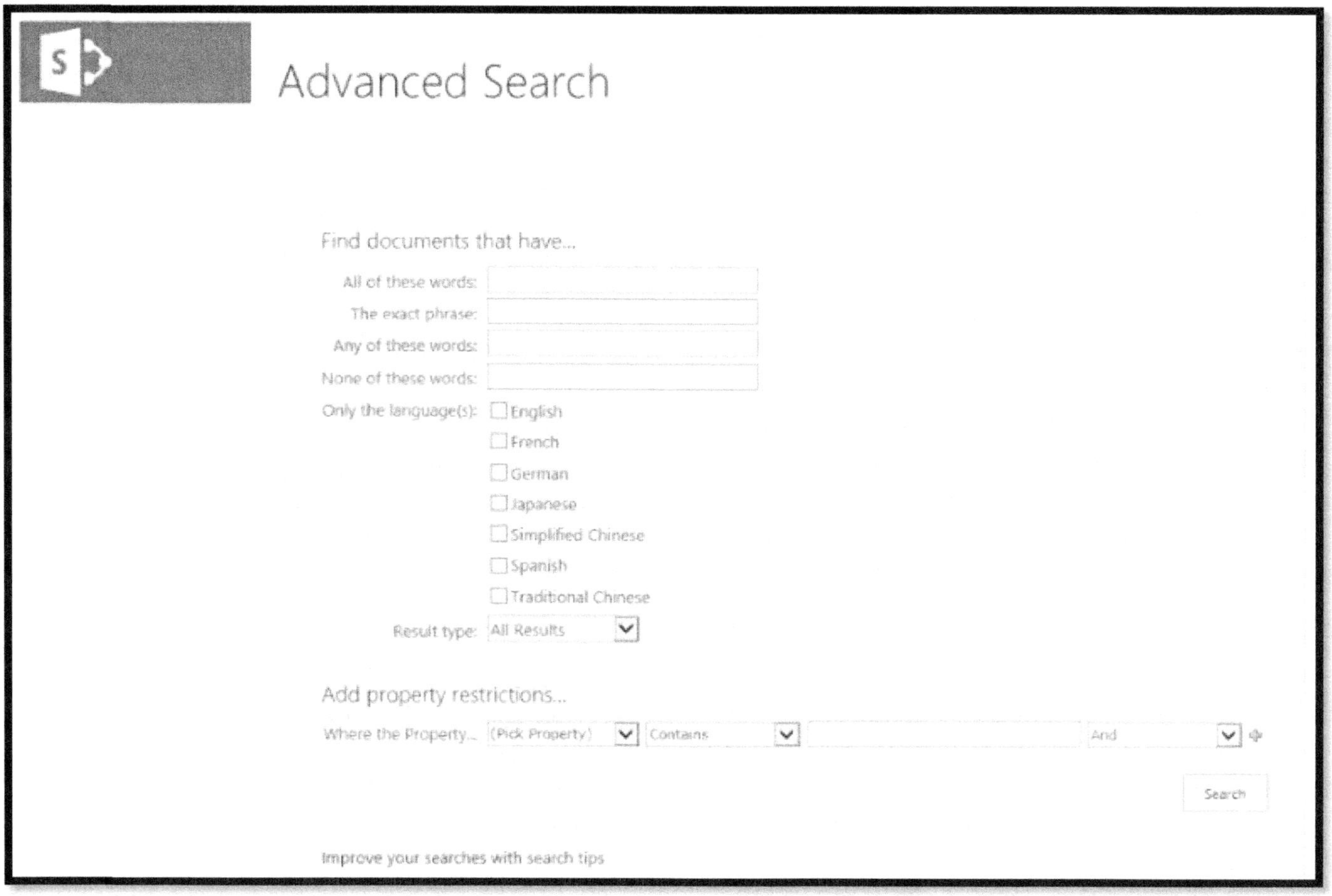

Access to your advanced search page is heavily influenced by how your administrators set up your search system. Searching for "Advanced Search" in a search boxset to search "**Everything**" should be the most efficient way to get there, and it should be the first result to appear.

Navigate to the bottom of any search results page and choose Advanced Search. This is yet another approach for reaching the page with sophisticated search options. To access advanced search, use this link: https://[domain].sharepoint.com/search/Pages/advanced.aspx. Use SharePoint Online to do your search.

Mark that website as a bookmark or favorite, and if you want to get there fast, ask your IT administrators to add a link to the com-pany's homepage.

Continuing with the last example, here is how to use advanced search to get the same result (which is really somewhat better). When this happens, the search returns results that meet the requirements specified below:

1. Use the words **"human resources"** and either "**benefits**" or "**insurance"** in their totality.
2. No files from 2015 will be included in the results. 4. Only documents (PDFs or Word documents) will be shown.
3. The file was last modified by someone with the surname "**Matt**" (e.g. "**Matthew**" or "Matthews "). This search will only return files that were last modified between January 1st and February 28th, 2016 (assuming the file was posted or changed in January or February).

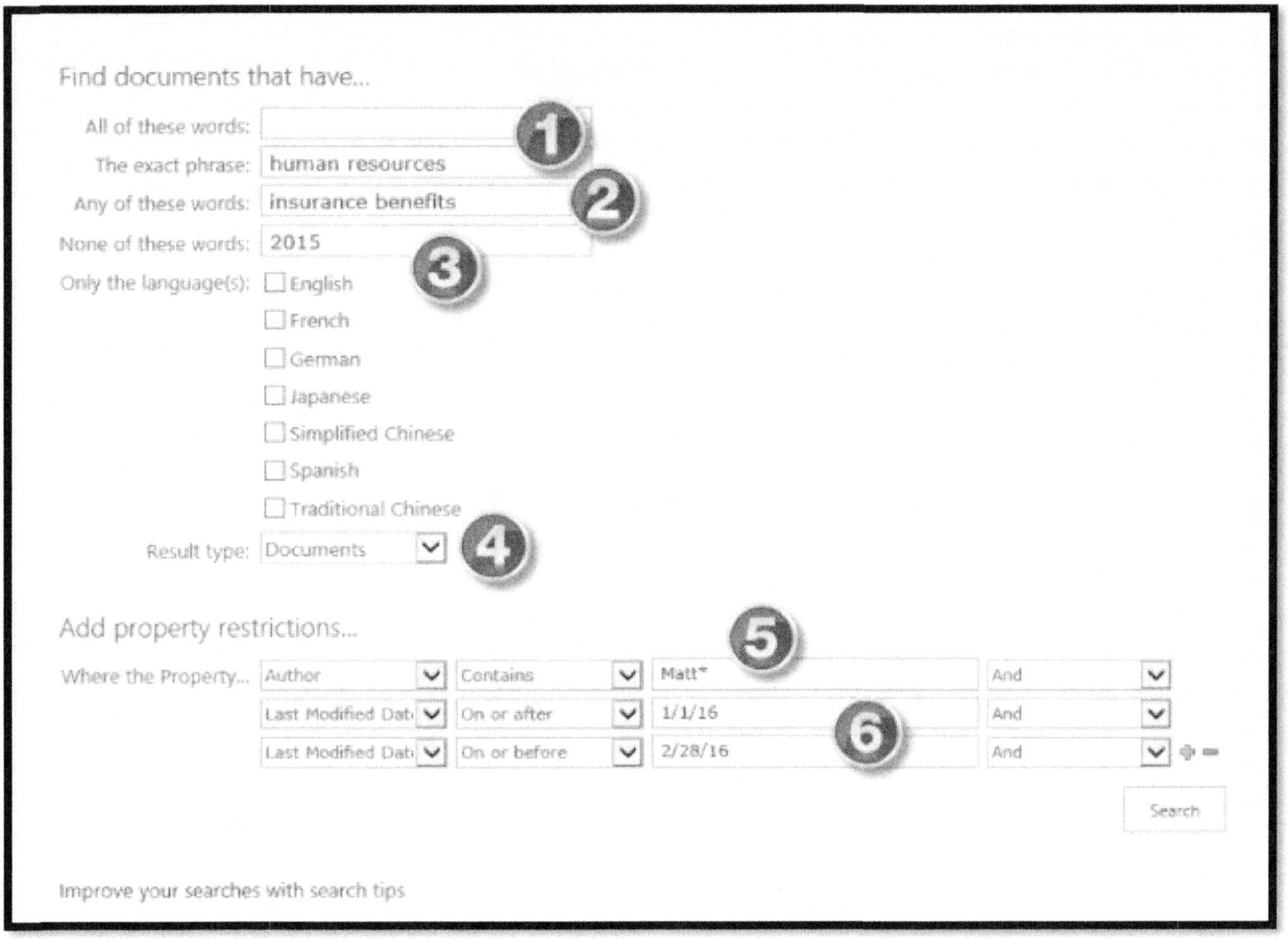

It is inconvenient that the language selection takes up so much space while working in a SharePoint system with people who only speak one language. It goes without saying that you will have to deal with it.

RESULTS REFINERS

Refiners are the most effective way to improve your outcomes. They allow you to restrict your results by excluding date ranges, file types, and authors that are irrelevant to your search.

You can either choose the author or file type for which you wish to view results, or you can alter the scale based on the modified date range. This eliminates unnecessary results while bringing more relevant information to the forefront.

The date refiner is logarithmic in nature. To put it another way, it is completely non-linear. Contrary to popular belief, the scale's points are not divided equally.

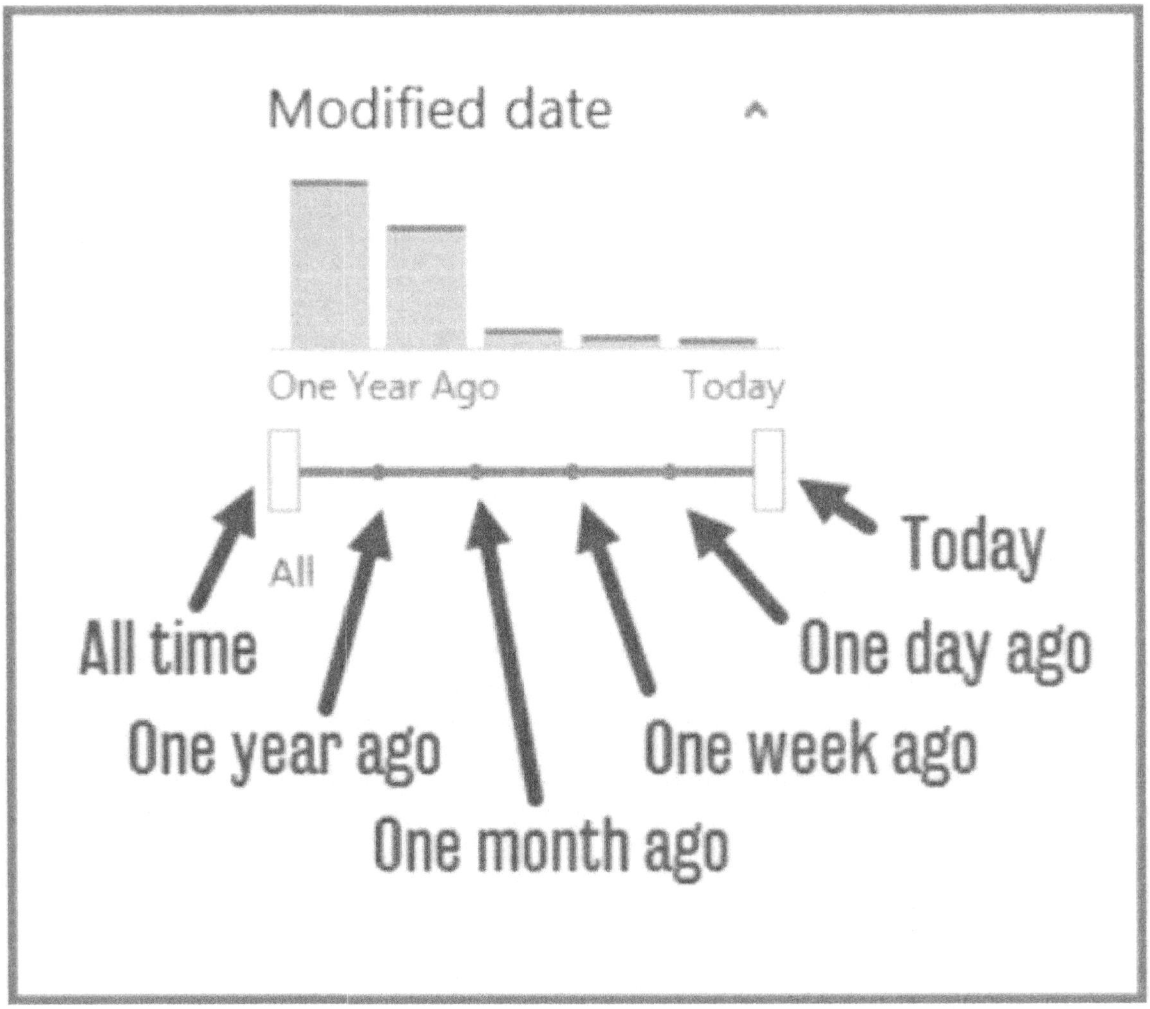

UNDERSTANDING THE QUERY SYNTAX FOR EFFECTIVE SEARCH

SharePoint search supports both Keyword Query Language (KQL) and FAST Query Language (FQL)search syntax.

KEYWORD QUERY LANGUAGE (KQL)

KQL is the query language used by default for creating search queries. The search keywords or property limitations provided to the SharePoint search service may be specified using KQL.

FAST QUERY LANGUAGE (FQL)

The FAST Query Language is a structured query language that supports the insertion of new query operators. The FQL language may be used to formulate complex searches that are then programmatically sent to the SharePoint search engine. End users should not be exposed to FQL, hence it is set to be deactivated by default.

To activate FQL set the Enable FQL property. After copying the default result source, modify the Query Transformation string{?{searchTerms} -ContentClass=urn:content-class:SPSPeople} at the SearchService Application (SSA), Site Collection, or Site levels:

- Remove the KQL filter (-ContentClass:urn:content-class:SPSPeople) from the Query Transformation.The final Query Transformationstring will be:{?{searchTerms}}
- Replace the Query Transformation string with the FQL equivalent:{?andnot({searchTerms},filter(content-class:"urn:contentclass:SPSPeople*"))}
.

CHAPTER 13: MANAGING PERMISSIONS

SHAREPOINT PERMISSIONS

There are four major kinds of permissions in SharePoint Online:

1. **Site Permissions**: Site permissions determine who may access a SharePoint site. Site permissions are often estab-lished at the root level, but they may also be configured at the subsite level.
2. **List Permissions:** List or library permissions determine who may see and modify a listor library in a SharePoint site. You can configure permissions for a SharePoint list at both the list and library levels.
3. **Folder Permissions**: In SharePoint Online, folder permissions function similarly to site or document library permis-sions. Users may have several levels of access to folders, such as Read, Contribute, or Full Control.
4. **Item Permissions:** Item permissions determine who may access and modify a specific item or document in a list or library. Items may have different permissions than lists, which can be configured at the document or list item level.

To set permissions for a site or item, you must be the site owner or have administrative access to the site. Permissions in SharePoint Online are configured at the site level and may be delegated to subsites, lists, libraries, and even single items inside those lists and libraries. Site administrators may establish permissions for it, and those permissions will apply to all of its subsites, lists, and li-braries unless special permissions are defined for a specific subsite, list, library, or item.

SHAREPOINT PERMISSION LEVELS

Permission levels in SharePoint Online determine what a person or group may do on a site, list, library, or item. Some permission levels are included with SharePoint Online, such as Full Control, Edit, and Read. However, if necessary, you can create your own per- mission levels.

SharePoint Online's default permission levels are:

- **Full Control:** This permission level allows users to see, add, update, and delete all material on the site, list, library, or item. Users with Full Control permissions may additionally edit user permissions or item-level security settings, cre-ate and delete libraries and lists, modify the site's design and feel, and manage site content, library, and list settings.
- **Design**: Edit content in a list, library, or item on the site. You can also create and delete lists and libraries with this level of permission. Some users have Design per mission s, which allow them to modify how the site appears and feels. However, they are unable to adjust the security settings for the site, a list, a library, or an item.
- **Edit:** This permission level allows users to read and update information on the site, list, library, or item. Users with Edit permissions are unable to update the security settings for a site, list, library, or item. By default, members of a SharePoint team site have this permission.

- **Contribute:** Users with this permission level can see and edit any information on the site, including items, lists, and libraries. However, they are unable to create or delete lists or libraries. SharePoint users with just the "Contribute " permissions cannot modify how the site appears or functions. They are also unable to adjust the security settings for the site, list, library, or item.
- **Read:** The Read permission level allows users to see site, library, list, or item content but cannot modify or delete it. Users with just Read permissions are unable to update the security settings for a site, list, library, or item. Most of the time, site users get it.
- **View Only:** Users with this permission level may only see information in the site, library, list, or item, but cannot add, alter, delete, or edit them. Users with "**View Only**" permissions are unable to change the security settings for the site, list, library, or item. They can browse sites, set alarms, and see items, but they cannot download files to client applications.

To create a custom permission level, follow these steps:

1. Navigate to the sit e's settings page to adjust permission levels.
2. Proceed to navigate to "**Settings,** "then "**Site Permissions**," and then "**Advanced Permission Settings.**"
3. On the Permissions page, choose the "**Permission levels**" link from the menu.
4. Select "**Adda Permission Level**" from the "Permission Levels" tab.
5. Identify the new permission level and describe its purpose.
6. Select specific permissions to add to the permission level. You can choose from a list of predefined permissions such as" **Full Control• "Edit," and "Read."** Choose the specific permissions that work best for you.
7. To create a new permission level, click the "**Create"** button.

After creating a unique permission level, you can assign it to individuals or security groups as appropriate.

COPY EXISTING PERMISSION LEVEL

You can create a new permission level in SharePoint by copying an existing one. Perform the tasks mentioned in steps 1- 3. You can also copy any current permission level, such as "**Contribute**," by selecting the "**Copy Permission Level**" button. You can then add or delete permissions such as "**Open items** ","**application pages**", **"Browse user information", "Personal web parts", "Client integra-tion features", "Remote interfaces**", and others.

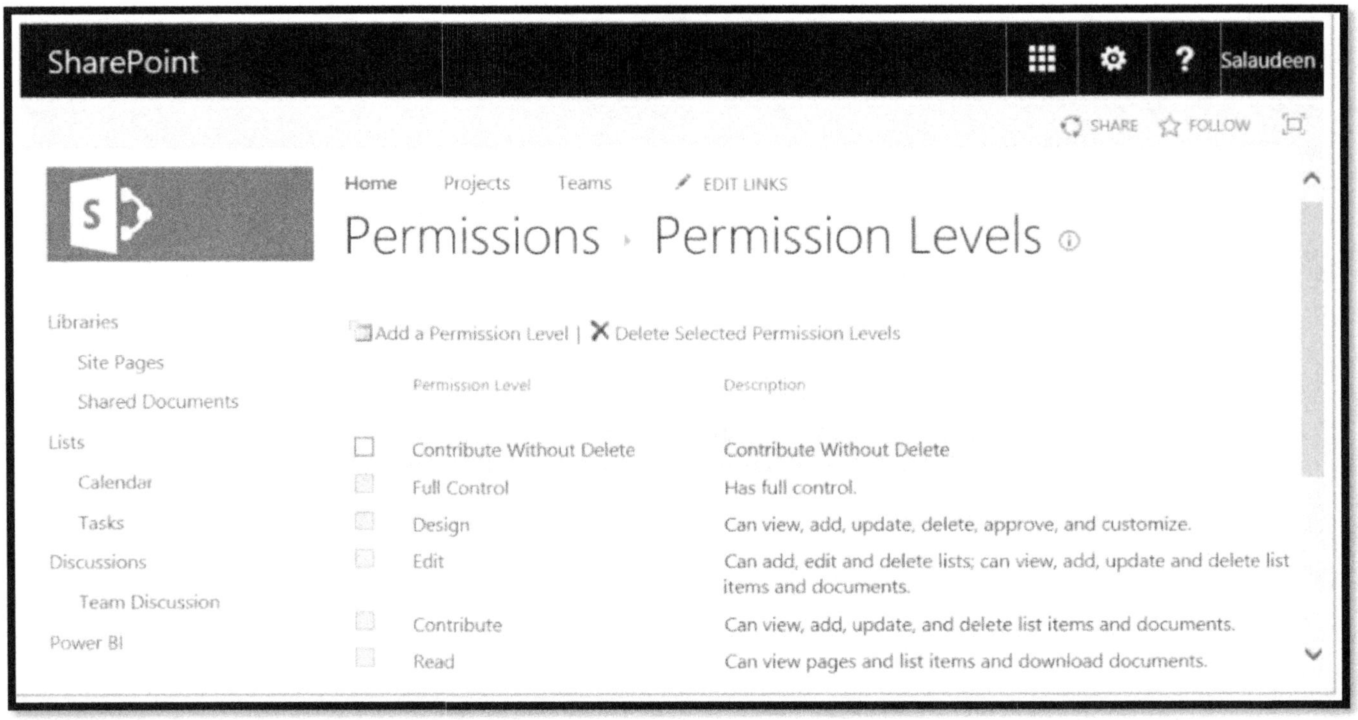

MANAGE PERMISSIONS IN SHAREPOINT ONLINE

There are numerous methods to configure and manage permissions in SharePoint Online.

1. **SharePoint Groups:** A group of users with the same permissions. Different groups may be formed for a variety of reasons, such as one for site managers and another for project team members. You can add or delete individuals from groups as you see fit, and any changes you make to the group's permissions will affect everyone in it.
2. **Individual Permissions:** Set permissions for individuals or groups on a list, library, or item. Individual permissions take precedence over permissions specified for a group or level of permission.

HOW CAN I MANAGE SHAREPOINT ONLINE PERMISSIONS?

In SharePoint Online, you update permissions using the user interface (UI). You can quickly add or delete individuals from your site or document library, assign them jobs and responsibilities, and create groups to manage several people at once. Each position has varying levels of permissions. For example, a supervisor will have greater control over the site than an ordinary user.

Private Team site vs. Public Team site

When you link a Microsoft 36 5 group to a SharePoint site, you can change the site's privacy to private or public. Th is indicates that only certain people can access the site, or that all users inside the firm may access it by adding them to SharePoint's special group **"Everyone except external users".**

DEFAULT GROUPS AND PERMISSIONS IN SHAREPOINT ONLINE

When you create a new team site or discussion site in SharePoint Online, a few basic SharePoint groups are created. These groups are used to regulate who can access the site and its content, as well as the permissions they have. Here's a list of fundamental groups and their permissions:

1. **The owners:** This group is in charge of the whole site and its content. They may make further changes to the site, such as adding and removing users and setting permissions.
2. **Members**: Members of this group can edit the site, add/remove content, create lists and libraries, and manage per- missions for their papers and other items.
3. **Visitors:** This group can only read the site's content. They can access any item on the site but cannot modify anything.
4. **Approvers:** This group can approve or reject submissions for review.
5. **Hierarchy Managers:** This group can create and manage sites and pages in the site collection.

Setup a SharePoint Group: In addition to these basic groups, you can create unique groups in SharePoint and provide them with the necessary permissions.

FOLDER LEVEL PERMISSIONS IN SHAREPOINT ONLINE

You can restrict who may see certain SharePoint folders. Sure! In SharePoint Online, you can manage who may view which files in a list or library by defining folder-level permissions. Users with read permissions to a list or library will have automatic access to all of its folders. However, you can use folder-level permissions to restrict access to select folders in the list or library to certain persons or security groups.

To establish group-level permissions in SharePoint Online, follow these steps:

1. Navigate to the folder's list or library to update its permissions.
2. Select the folder you want to update the permissions for.
3. Select the **"Files"** tab from the ribbon. Then click the "**Manage Access**" option.
4. In the "**Manage Access**" box, add persons or SharePoint security groups and assign appropriate permission levels. To remove a person or security group from the list, click the" **X** "next to their name.
5. Once you've specified permissions, click the **"Save"** button to apply the changes.

Keep in mind that SharePoint folder permissions differ from list and library permissions. If you want a user or security group to be able to see all of the files in a list or library, you must grant them permission at the list or library level. These steps may be completed by adding the person or group to the list of individuals and groups with permissions on the list or the library's "**Permissions**" page.

HOW TO GRANT ACCESS TO A DOCUMENT IN SHAREPOINT?

It is also possible to provide permissions to particular items in a list or library. This comes in helpful when some items in a list or library need different permissions than others. How do I allow someone in SharePoint to see a certain file? To set permissions for a single item, the owner must first disable permissions from the parent list or library. Once the inheritance is broken, the supervisor may add persons and groups to the item and provide them with specific permissions.

Here's how to set permissions at the file level in SharePoint Online:

1. Locate the file or folder you want to adjust permissions for.
2. Select the file and click the "**Share**" button. This will display the "**Share With Others**" box.
3. Enter the email address of the individual or group to establish permissions in the "**Invite People**" box.
4. Select the appropriate entrance level from the "**Permission Level**" selection menu.
5. Optionally, provide a statement with your request. Enter it into the "**Add a message(optional)**" box.
6. To send the invite and specify permissions, use the "**Share"** option.

Remember that the precise file-level permissions you can use may vary depending on how your company has configured Share- Point. If you need to establish permissions that are not available in the "Permission Level" menu, you may need to request addi-tional permissions from your supervisor.

HOW TO CHECK USER PERMISSIONS IN SHAREPOINT ONLINE?

You may need to periodically verify who has what permissions on a SharePoint Online site. This is especially crucial when you have a large number of workers with various occupations. Let's look at how to verify permissions on SharePoint.

Here's how to verify site permissions in SharePoint Online:

1. Go to the SharePoint site to verify permissions.
2. In the upper right corner of the page, choose the "**Settings**" option. From the menu that appears, choose "**Site settings**."
3. On the "**Site Settings**" tab, go to **"Users and Permissions"** and choose the **"Site permissions"** link.
4. The "**Site permissions"** page displays a list of users and security groups having access to the site, including their per- mission levels.

To verify permissions on a library or list, use the same steps: In the list, choose the name of the list or library. This will bring up a window displaying the precise permissions granted to the list or library. Please bear in mind that viewing the site, list, or library permissions requires that you already have the necessary permissions.

ANONYMOUS ACCESS IN SHAREPOINT ONLINE

If you change your external sharing settings to **"Anyone**," you can share a file or folder with anybody in secret. Anyone who has the link to a file or folder that you have shared privately may open it without entering your password.

To share a file or folder on SharePoint Online with individuals other than yourself, follow these steps:

1. Open SharePoint Online and choose the file or folder to share.
2. Right-click the item and choose the **"Share"** option.
3. In the link settings, choose **"Anyone with the link"** and provide the recipients' email addresses.
4. Select the appropriate permissions for private users, such as Edit and View, from the drop-down box.
5. Select "**Send**."

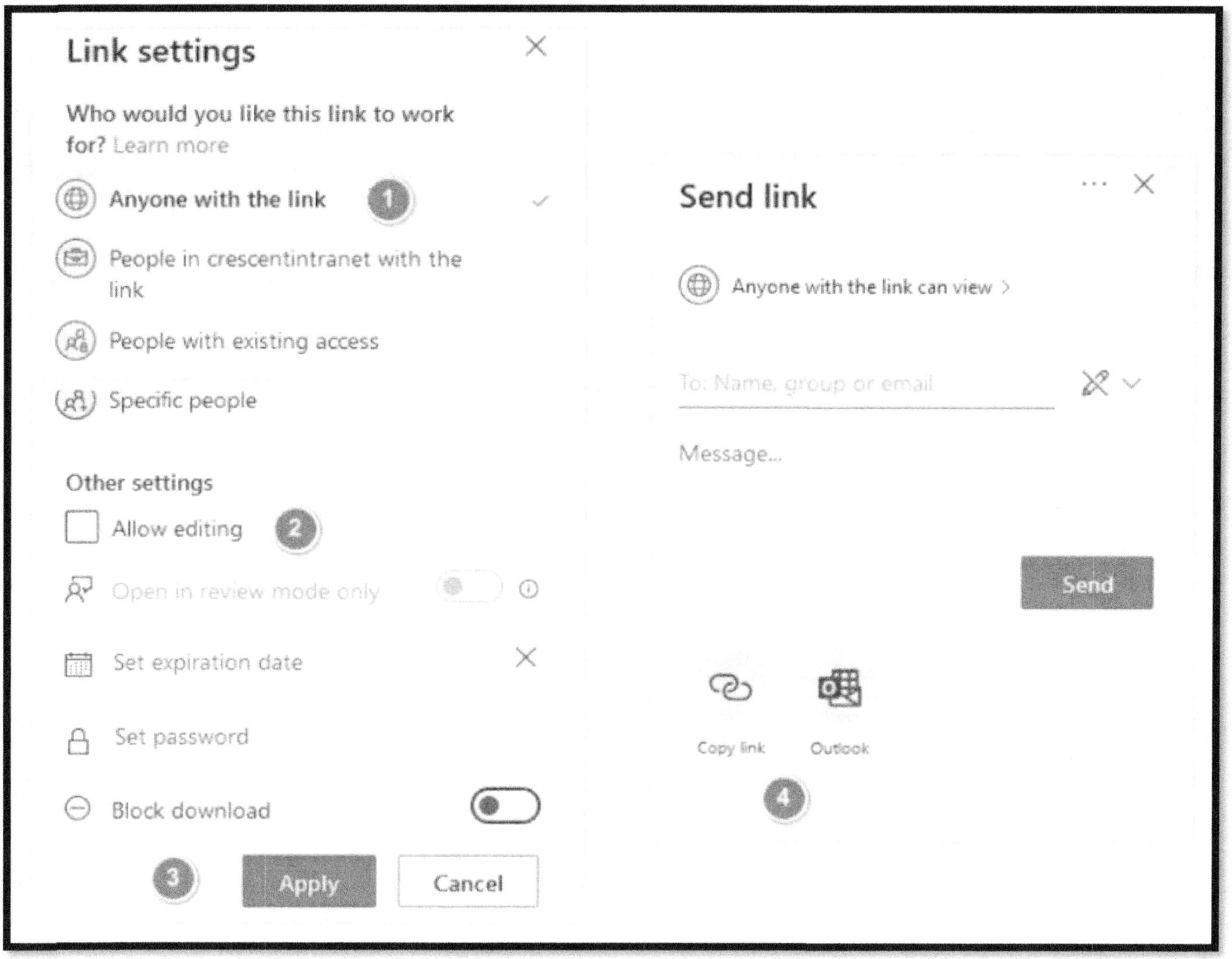

This will generate a unique link that you can share with individuals you don't know and allow them to access the file or folder via that link.

CHAPTER 14: ENSURING SHAREPOINT SECURITY

MANAGING SHAREPOINT ONLINE SECURIT: A TEAM EFFORT

Tenant settings

This is where you should start before allowing users to access SharePoint. Unfortunately, most customers start using the platform with the default settings remaining in place.

However, you need to pay close attention to a few tenant settings. The sharing settings are quite crucial. They may have disastrous consequences and trigger data breaches if left to their own devices. Let us begin with this scenario.

Sharing settings

To access tenant-level sharing settings, go to the SharePoint Admin Center and click on **Sharing** under **Policies.**

The fact that SharePoint and OneDrive are ranked on the same level as the term **"Anyone"** should be the first thing that raises your pulse rate. Isn't it strange that individuals may exchange folders and files using links that do not need the other person to sign in? Any recipient will do.

You should immediately slide down one level unless you're certain you want to stay there.

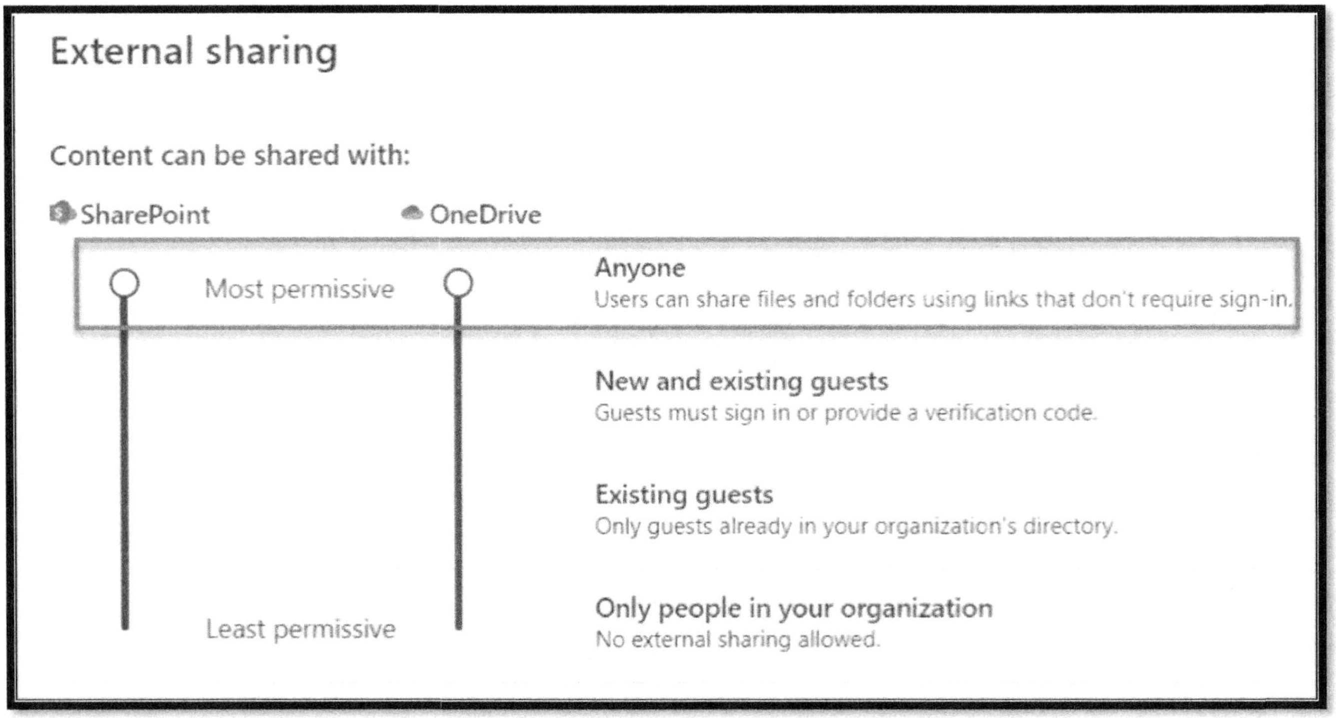

At this stage, you don't even need to know the specific OneDrive for Business policies for your company. Furthermore, the Share- Point option will cause the scale to go down one level. Because individuals cannot share more easily on OneDrive for Business than on SharePoint.

Once you know the corporate policy, you may choose the appropriate sharing settings from the following:

- New and existing guests
- Existing guests
- Only people in your organization

More external sharing settings

Once again, there are some options to assist us acquire a bit more if necessary. You may choose any or all of them. However, just because you can does not mean you should!

Limit external sharing by domain. If you choose this option, you may allow or block certain websites. Working with specific con-sumers or partners is a common occurrence. This parameter may be changed at both the renter and site levels.

Keep in mind that clicking **"Allow"** on one or more of the other sites will result in their blocking. Even if you **"Block"** some of the names, the others will be able to connect.

Only allow personnel in certain Security Groups to share with others outside the company: If selected, only members of the private group(s) will be allowed to communicate with those outside the group.

This option will only be accessible if the tenant's sharing settings are set to **"New and Existing Guests"** or "b

Guests must log in with the same account that was used to issue the sharing invites. As an added layer of security, this ensures that the person viewing the file(s) is the person you want to have access to. If possible, you should choose this option.

People who use a verification code must confirm their identification again after [number of days): A new method has been imple-mented in which visitors will enter a one-time PIN to log in for the number of days they choose.

Site settings

SharePoint permissions are such a large topic that it's difficult to focus on anything else. And problems don't improve when sites are connected together in groups!

Consider permissions to be a peak. The procedure begins at the top (site level), and as we go down, we may assign them to papers one by one.

SharePoint Groups

It makes no difference whether the site is group-connected or not; when you create a site (depending on the design), three Share- Point groups are automatically created:

- Owners.
- Members.

- Visitors.

Each built-ingroup has a certain permission level. You should utilize them initially, but if they don't work for you, create a new SharePoint group and provide your permission level.

You can clone a permission level and choose which options to use or not use based on your requirements. If necessary, create your own SharePoint group and permission level. Do not modify or remove the built-in groups.

Active Directory (AD) Groups

Most firms currently have an Active Directory on their premises that is connected to Microsoft 365. When granting permissions to a SharePoint site, security groups should be added to the SharePoint groups.

You may, however, create Microsoft 365 security groups in the admin center and add them to your SharePoint site. SharePoint groups are not identical to Active Directory groups. If you create a SharePoint group, it will only be visible on the site where it was created.

Adding security groups to your SharePoint groups is the greatest way to get control. It is feasible to add individuals to sites one at a time, but doing so will make it more difficult to monitor them in the future.

Breaking permission inheritance

At certain times, you may need to allow someone to utilize merely a library or a document rather than the whole site. That is where we may prevent permissions from being handed down. This is more the responsibility of the Site Owner than the Site Member.

When you create a website and begin to construct libraries, lists, and share documents, everyone who visits the site has access to those libraries and documents. Remember that stuff about the crescendo?

When eliminating permission transfer after creating the library or list, the typical SharePoint groups (i.e., Owners, Members, Visi- tors) will remain visible in the site permissions settings. Add your account (to maintain access), then delete the default SharePoint groups and add everyone who requires access to this library, which now has unique permissions.

Site Sharing

Sharing on your website will change if it is not tied to a Microsoft 365 Group. The redesigned design allows you to manage permis-sions more effectively and provides additional sharing possibilities.

Sites are not linked to Microsoft 365 groups

If your site is not affiliated to a group, little has changed. Even though the UI has been updated,

SharePoint professionals will still know how to share a site and utilize the Advanced Permissions Settings.

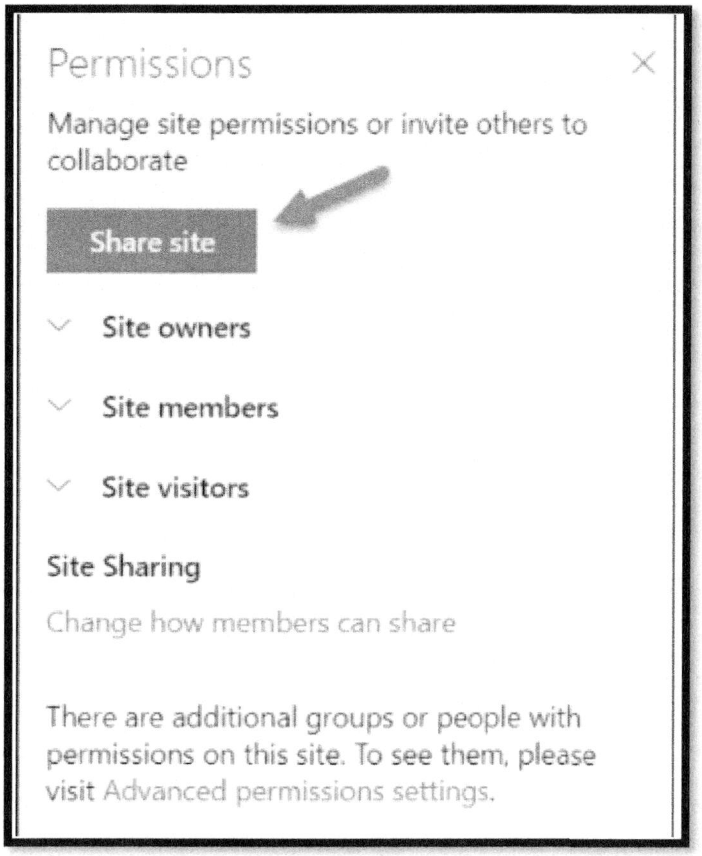

Sites connected to Microsoft 365 groups

You can still share the Site Only after joining a group. In other words, you are not required to use any other Microsoft 365 group tools, such as a shared email, Planner, etc.

Then, select **Invite people > Add members to the group** if you want to share the site, add users to the group, and the user(s) will be included in all of the Microsoft 365 group functions.

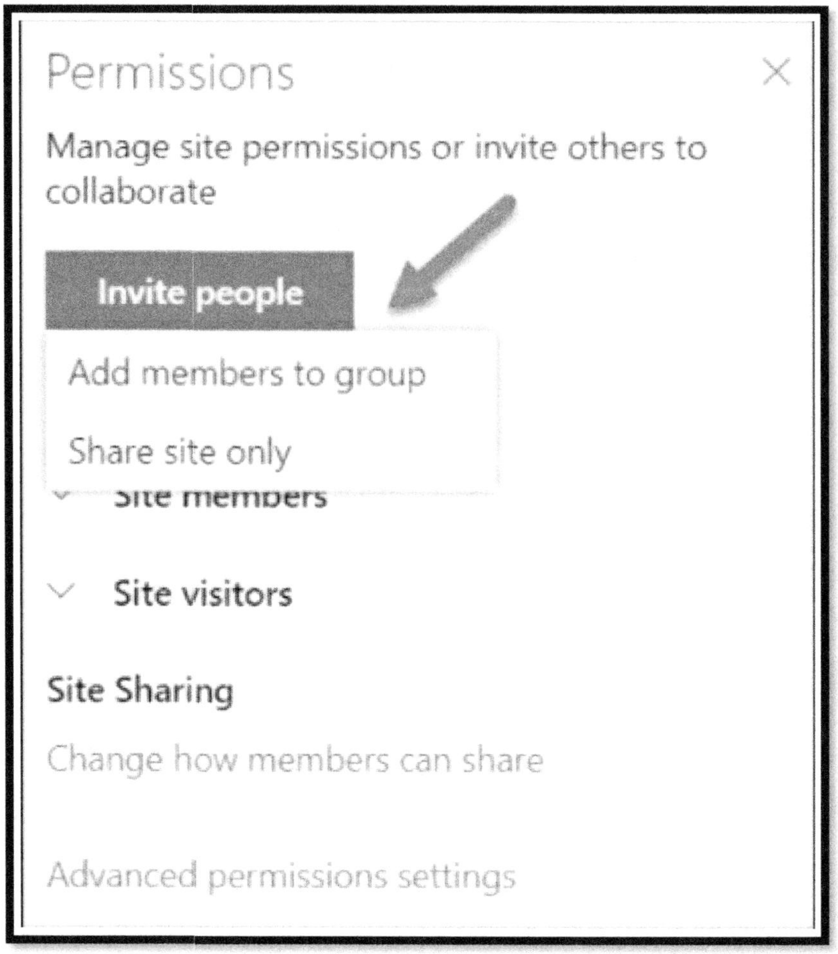

CHANGE HOW MEMBERS CAN SHARE

Another factor that may reduce the likelihood of sharing is the ability to choose between the following three options:

- Members and site owners may share files, folders, and even the whole site. Any user with Edit permissions may ac-cess shared files and folders.
- Members, site owners, and those with Edit permissions can share files and folders, but only site owners can share the site itself.
- Only site owners can share folders, files, and the whole site.

The only difference between the first two bullet points is that option 2 allows just the site owner to share the site. Members will not do it.

The third bullet point is quite obvious, but we can understand how it may get in the way of individuals completing their jobs. What if you have something to tell a colleague or a customer? Also, this will make the site owner's work more difficult...

This option might be used if your users are new to SharePoint, if they need further training before sharing with confidence, or if you just do not want them to share at all.

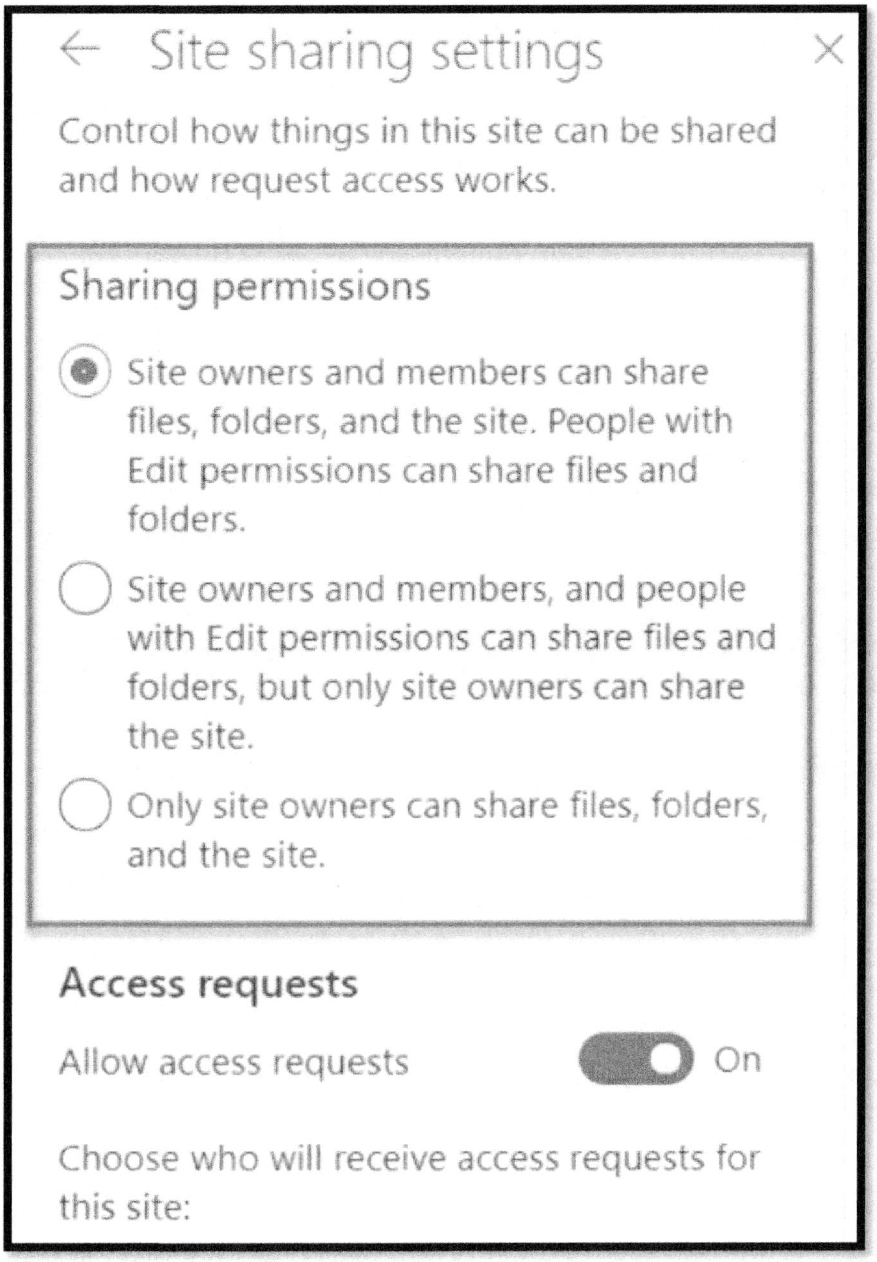

ACCESS REQUESTS

As you can see in the image above, Access Requests were enabled by default. This functionality has been available for a long and is preferable to receiving the unpleasant "Access denied" notification, which you can't do anything about. It is still not completely configured in SharePoint on-premises, but everything is ready to use on SharePoint Online. We only need to pick who should get those requests, compose a customized message to the individual making the request, and then review the open requests again.

There are two possibilities for who should receive access requests:

- Site Owners
- Specific email addresses

CHAPTER 15: DISASTER RECOVERY AND BACKUP STRATEGIES

UNDERSTANDING SHAREPOINT BACKUP

SharePoint backups are essential for every organization. Protecting and recovering your data in the event of a failure. There are various options for backing up: SharePoint's tool, third-party programs, or doing it manually. Prior to beginning the procedure, the SharePoint farm, files, and settings must all be thoroughly backed up. A robust backup strategy keeps your organization running and prevents you from losing data.

When creating a plan, consider how often, what kind of backup (full or partial), where to store the data, and how long to retain it. Always verify your copies to ensure they are accurate. If necessary, you may consult a professional since the basic method may not completely back up certain aspects.

Plan and implement a SharePoint backup plan to keep the company functioning smoothly. Don't be concerned about losing your SharePoint information; instead, take care of it and back it up.

DIFFERENT METHODS FOR PROTECTING YOUR SHAREPOINT DATA

Your SharePoint data will be secure as long as you use backup strategies. Here are some tried-and-true methods for keeping your SharePoint settings secure.

- **Full Back up option:** This option saves the site's content, settings, and permissions to a backup file.
- **Differential Backup:** Tracks changes since the previous complete backup.
- **Incremental Backup:** Tracks changes to site collections since the last full or partial backup.
- **Granular Backup:** This sort of backup covers specific SharePoint sites, lists, and document stores.

You can also back your SharePoint data using third-party technologies like Cloud Ally, Veeam, and AvePoint, or you can utilize the tools included with SharePoint. It is critical to test the backup and recovery processes regularly to ensure that stored files can be re-trieved and utilized in an emergency.

Full Farm Backup

SharePoint is perfect for team communication and data management. Backup your SharePoint data regularly to ensure its security. You can choose the "**Full Farm Backup**" option.

1. Visit the Central Administration's website. Click on "**Back Up and Restore.**"
2. Click "**Start Backup**" after selecting "**Farm Backup.**"
3. Select a place to store the backup file.
4. Check your settings. Click "**Back Up Now**."

Be patient, as full farm backup takes time. Following these steps, you will have completed the backup. Schedule backups for periods of inactivity, such as when you are not working. To ensure safety, save the backup copy someplace else. SharePoint Health Analyzer is being used to monitor for any issues or alarms.

If you do this, your SharePoint information will be protected. Granular backup takes a long time, but it's worthwhile in the end.

Granular Backup

Granular backups are required for SharePoint to function properly. It protects data and saves time and space. To do this, you can use PowerShell or Central Adrnin, both of which are included within SharePoint. You can also use third-party backup programs, which are more user-friendly.

Granular backup allows you to back up individual lists, books, websites, and even papers. Customized rules and plans may allow it to operate autonomously. It reduces the likelihood of data loss. Furthermore, cloud-based services such as Microsoft 365 provide the capability to create very thorough backups.

Note: Make sure to test your backups often. It will guarantee that things are resolved in a circumstance.

Backup Via PowerShell

Do you want to save a copy of your SharePoint data? PowerShell from Microsoft is the solution! This program is robust and adapt- able, and it has a command-line interface for rapid operations. Let's look at how to use PowerShell to create a solid backup.

1. Use "**Add-PSSnapin Microsoft.SharePoint Powershell**" in Windows PowerShell to access SharePoint.
2. Select the site group or subsite you wish to save. The command **"New-Item E:\ Backup -type directory**" creates a new backup folder.
3. To create a backup object, use cmdlets such as Backup-SPFarm, Backup-SPConfiguration Database, or Export-SPWeb.
4. Choose whether to use full or split backup.
5. To start the backup process, use **"Backup-SPFarm-Directory E:\ Backup-BackupMethod Full".**

If you want to back up many subsites or collections of sites, repeat steps 2, 3, 4, and 5. PowerShell allows you to easily monitor SharePoint data backups while keeping them small enough to store and retrieve. These measures help you feel comfortable and save time in the event of an emergency. Don't allow terrible things to to happen to Simple Things Publishing; use PowerShell to back up SharePoint now.

Third-Party Backup Solutions

Third-party backup alternatives may have functionality that SharePoint's backup tools do not. With these choices, you can back up and restore everything, as well as back up individual files or sections of files. There are other options for automatic scheduling and reporting, as well as more detailed information about the status and performance of backups.

When selecting a third-party backup solution, consider how simple it is to use, how scalable it is, and how well it integrates with other systems. You may select from Commvault Complete Backup & Recovery for SharePoint, Veeam Backup & Replication for Mi-crosoft SharePoint, and Druva in Sync for SharePoint.

Overall, these sophisticated capabilities prevent your SharePoint data from being accidentally deleted or destroyed in unexpected ways. Don't forget to back up SharePoint. It's like keeping your ex's phone number on hand in case you need it.

BEST PRACTICES IN SHAREPOINT BACKUP

Keeping backups of SharePoint data is critical for keeping the organization operational. Best Practices for SharePoint Backup are required for backup and disaster recovery plans.

Here are our thoughts on SharePoint Backup:

- Create a backup strategy to ensure frequent backups.
- Use incremental backups rather than full backups to reduce backup time and size;
- Run a restore job on the backup data to confirm backup accuracy;
- Store multiple backup copies in different locations to reduce data loss;
- Set up security protocols to prevent unauthorized access and encrypt backups for privacy.

SharePoint Backup contains many twists and turns, such as how to manage lost data and deleted sites. It is critical to thoroughly understand these changes if you wish to create SharePoint Backup rules that are effective and helpful.

Determine Backup Frequency

Back up your SharePoint data in case of a calamity, system failure, or accidental loss. Det er m in e how often you should back up your data based on its worth and frequency of change.

- **Daily backups** are recommended for frequent changes.
- **Weekly backups** are sufficient for information that does not change often.
- **Monthly backups** will save time and space for data that changes infrequently.
- Backups at **quarterly, half-yearly**, and **annual intervals**. Less-u sed data should be backed up every three, six, or twelve months for legal purposes or storage.

Keep many copies of your backup offline in case of a fire, storm, or other natural catastrophe. Confirm that the backup provider can restore all of SharePoint's content, not just certain files.

Store Backups Securely

To keep your SharePoint system secure and operational, backups must be kept in a secure place. Encrypting files and keeping them in a secure place are two fundamental strategies to do this. Role-based access control may be used to increase security by allowing only those who are supposed to be there in.

To defend against data loss due to technical failure or calamities, several copies should be kept in various secure sites. Also, testing the backup technique often ensures that it will operate well when required. If you follow these best practices for SharePoint backup storage, you can be certain that no one else will have access to your data without your permission and that it will be protected if anything unexpected occurs.

Backup and recovery systems are similar to relationships in that you won't know whether they function until it's too late.

Test Backup and Restore Processes

To ensure data access and reliability, test your backup and recovery procedures. Use this as a guide.

- Copy your actual settings in the test environment.
- Generate fake data for testing.
- Back up the test place completely.
- Remove one or more phony sets.
- Recover lost information from the complete backup.
- Test the returned data to ensure it works properly.

Don't assume that your backups functioned just because they were completed. Include and test your emergency rescue strategies. Conduct random exercises as part of your normal testing regimen. Prepare for awful things to happen; you never know when they will.

In one situation, a corporation was surprised when its server collapsed. Some of the files they attempted to restore from backups were corrupted or destroyed, therefore the operation failed. Instead of completing crucial work, they spent hours fixing outdated files. This may have been prevented by testing often.

Backing up SharePoint settings is like wearing a helmet when riding a bike: it is painful but necessary to prevent a crash.

BACKUP SHAREPOINT CONFIGURATION

Backing up your SharePoint configuration files is essential for seamless functioning.

Here's how you can accomplish this:

1. Go to **Administrative Tools** in the Start Menu and choose **SharePoint Central Administration.**
2. Select "**Backup and Restore**" from the left menu. Then click "**Performa backup."**
3. Select "**Farm Backup**" from the "**Backup Options**" tab. In Farm Selection, choose all of the components. Choose "**Full**" as the type and a backup plan.
4. To prevent data loss, backup systems must be kept up to date. Give each backup a name so you don't unintentionally erase another one.

RESTORE SHAREPOINT FROM BACKUP

Because of how much we rely on technology these days, all companies must back up their data. SharePoint, a popular document management and collaboration platform, has been added. In the case of unexpected data loss or destruction, swiftly retrieving backup data is critical.

These six basic steps will restore SharePoint from a backup:

1. To start the backup, open **SharePoint Central Administration** on the server where it was created.
2. Go to Backup and Restore, choose **Restore from Backup**, and locate the backup file.
3. Select a healing point and the site group to bring back.
4. Recover specific elements of the backup, such as lists, libraries, and permissions.
5. Select repair options, including **"overwrite file"** and "create new sites."
6. To complete the repair procedure, click **OK**.

It is critical to periodically backup your SharePoint data and the components that are attached to it. Another thing to consider is developing a corporate disaster recovery strategy. This kind of strategy may involve having an off-site data storage option, verify-ing files for correctness, and backing up and testing disaster recovery procedures right immediately.

The only way to ensure that the SharePoint restoration process works is to update and verify files on a regular basis, even on days when there is minimal movement. A cloud-based backup and emergency recovery solution is worth considering since it is more flexible and accessible.

Finally; implement conventional company security procedures to safeguard backup data from risks such as those found online. If you need to restore SharePoint from a full-farm backup, keep in mind that, just as there is no place like home, there is no place like an up-to-date backup.

Restore from the Full Farm Backup

To ensure the security of your data, perform these four steps to restore SharePoint from a full farm backup:

1. Ensure you have the necessary accounts and permissions.
2. In Central Administration, choose "**Backup and Restore**" from the System Settings menu.
3. To restore your farm, choose "**Restore from Backup**" and locate the entire backup file.
4. Rest ore specific portions, confirm the right settings, and begin the recovery process.

Keep in mind that this may take some time, depending on how many files you have. Check and test your backups on a regular basis to ensure you are prepared when needed.

Before attempting to repair corrupted data, consider restoring from a backup. According to SharePoint documentation, this proce-dure maybe used to restore a farm to its original form after a catastrophe. However, incomplete backups may bring Share Point back to life like a bug.

Restore from Granular Backup

Recovering from Granular Backup for SharePoint involves three steps:

1. Access the backup folder for the selected group of sites.
2. Transfer site files to their proper location in SharePoint.

3. Conduct a thorough search for the source of the information.

Make sure that item-level restorations do not destroy any existing features. Granular saves provide several options. They can recover certain information and things without disrupting the rest. This allows administrators to recover lists or documents that were accidentally deleted.

Restore Via PowerShell

You can quickly restore SharePoint from a backup using PowerShell. It requires a great deal of expertise, but it ensures that all of your information and settings are restored.

Here's how you can do so:

1. Log in as an administrator to SharePoint Management Shell.
2. Enter the following: Restore-SPFarm -Directory **"Path to Backup Folder"**- Restore Method Overwrite -Item **Restore Type**. 'Restore Type' might refer to an online software, a content database, or a group of websites.
3. Select "Enter" and wait for the fix to be completed.

You must have sufficient diskspace and be able to go to the destination place. Each restoration has unique requirements based on the size of the backup, the amount of free space available, and the location of the disk.

A senior worker once used PowerShell to restore a database containing an essential document library. After two hours, he was over- joyed that nothing had gone wrong and that no data had been lost or destroyed. He is now even more convinced that PowerShell is an excellent tool for SharePoint admins. If you need to restore SharePoint from a third-party backup, it's like having a superhero on your side. They aren't always necessary, but when they are, they save lives.

CONCLUSION

In reflecting on the knowledge and tools provided throughout this guide, it's clear that SharePoint is far more than just a document storage or collaboration tool—it is a strategic asset capable of reshaping the way organizations function, communicate, and manage information. By now, you've taken the essential first steps toward mastering SharePoint, and you're equipped with the foundational knowledge to navigate, utilize, and even customize it to your needs. This guide has covered a breadth of topics, each essential to understanding and implementing SharePoint effectively, and it's this versatility that makes it one of the most powerful platforms available today for organizational efficiency and teamwork.

Learning to use SharePoint as a beginner involves more than just understanding its menus and features; it requires a shift in how you approach collaboration and information sharing within your organization. SharePoint operates as a digital hub, a central location where documents, communications, and processes converge. For many, this shift can transform work routines, bringing order to the complexity of managing content and improving the ability to access critical information quickly. As organizations grow and become more complex, SharePoint's centralized approach can help reduce information silos, bringing team members closer together through a shared workspace where ideas, updates, and resources are readily available.

A fundamental takeaway from this guide is that SharePoint is customizable to meet the unique needs of any user or organization. As you've seen, from setting up document libraries to managing permissions, SharePoint provides a variety of tools that make it adaptable and scalable. Whether you work in a small team or a large enterprise, you now have the knowledge to shape SharePoint into a personalized tool that suits specific tasks and projects. Customization isn't just about changing the look and feel of SharePoint; it's about creating a tailored environment where you and your team can work more effectively. It's about aligning SharePoint's capabilities with the workflows, requirements, and branding standards unique to your organization. This level of flexibility not only enhances productivity but also encourages engagement among team members who feel that the tools they use truly support their work.

Equipped with a solid understanding of SharePoint's navigation, libraries, lists, and customization options, you're now better prepared to tackle some of the more advanced features that will undoubtedly become valuable as you deepen your experience. From mobile access and integration to advanced search capabilities, SharePoint allows you to expand your engagement and become more efficient in locating, managing, and sharing content. In an era where the need for remote work and digital collaboration is constantly increasing, SharePoint's accessibility across devices ensures that you and your team are always connected. You now understand how to harness these features to maintain continuity and flexibility, regardless of where you're working from.

Beyond functionality, a key consideration in SharePoint is security, and by mastering permissions and access management, you've taken the necessary steps to ensure that your organization's information remains protected. Every organization has sensitive information that needs safeguarding, and SharePoint's security protocols allow you to control who can see, edit, and share specific content. By carefully managing permissions, you're contributing to an environment where trust and data integrity are upheld, and users feel confident in the safety of their information. Moreover, an understanding of SharePoint's security settings is crucial for regulatory compliance, making sure that your organization adheres to necessary privacy standards and guidelines.

As you move forward in your SharePoint journey, consider the importance of building a structure that supports long-term growth and adaptability. Document management, for example, should be approached as a living system, one that evolves with the changing needs of your organization. Using version control, metadata, and file organization, you can maintain order in a system that can otherwise become overwhelming with content over time. SharePoint empowers you to create a sustainable document management strategy, helping ensure that information is accessible not just for current projects but for future reference as well. By implementing best practices now, you're setting up a robust framework that will support your team's work in the years to come.

Another key area this guide has emphasized is collaboration. The tools within SharePoint aren't just designed to store information but to foster a collaborative environment. Whether it's through co-authoring documents, sharing updates on team sites, or utilizing task lists to track project progress, SharePoint enables real-time interaction and alignment. This means that team members can contribute ideas, update files, and communicate seamlessly within one shared platform. Effective collaboration drives productivity, and by integrating SharePoint into your team's daily routine, you're helping create a more cohesive, connected work culture. Over time, this will contribute to a sense of ownership and unity as team members engage more actively with each other and with the projects they're working on.

One of the most powerful aspects of SharePoint is its search and content discovery features, which allow users to quickly locate information amidst vast amounts of data. Understanding how to use SharePoint's search functionality effectively can save time and reduce frustration. By leveraging advanced search, metadata, and tagging, users can retrieve relevant content with ease, even as the volume of information grows. This functionality is especially critical in organizations where multiple projects, departments, and teams operate simultaneously. By taking advantage of SharePoint's search tools, you ensure that no matter how complex the information landscape becomes, you have the tools to navigate it efficiently.

In closing, SharePoint represents more than just a suite of tools; it represents a way to transform work processes and build a shared digital workspace that supports your organization's vision and goals. For those beginning with SharePoint, there's a learning curve, but the rewards are well worth the effort. The skills you've gained in this guide will not only improve your immediate productivity but will lay the groundwork for long-term success as you continue to grow within the SharePoint environment.

This journey with SharePoint may have started with an aim to master the basics, but as you continue, you'll find that each feature, each tool, and each customization option adds another layer of capability to your work. The platform's flexibility allows for continual learning and adaptation, ensuring that SharePoint remains relevant as your organization's needs change. With a solid foundation in the essential functions of SharePoint, you're now prepared to explore the platform's more advanced possibilities. In time, you'll discover additional ways to streamline processes, facilitate communication, and ultimately, contribute to a more productive and collaborative organization.

As you look ahead, remember that SharePoint's value lies in its capacity to evolve alongside your organization. Each step you take in mastering its tools will enhance your team's ability to work efficiently, communicate effectively, and manage information securely. This guide has provided the starting point, but the possibilities are vast, limited only by the creativity and ambition you bring to your SharePoint experience. With each new feature you explore and each process you optimize, you're contributing to a foundation of innovation and efficiency that will serve you and your organization well into the future.

In sum, this guide has given you the practical knowledge to approach SharePoint with confidence. You've gained insights into everything from basic navigation and mobile access to advanced permissions and disaster recovery. The investment you've made in learning these concepts will pay dividends, not only in your day-to-day tasks but in your ability to drive meaningful change in how your team collaborates and manages information. Remember, SharePoint is a tool that grows in value the more it is utilized and understood. As you continue to work within this platform, let your knowledge expand alongside it, discovering new ways to maximize its potential and make your mark in the digital workspace.

With SharePoint as a part of your professional toolkit, you're now positioned to lead, innovate, and contribute to a smarter, more connected future for your team and organization. This guide has merely been the beginning; the journey ahead will reveal even more possibilities as you apply these concepts and continue exploring the depths of SharePoint's capabilities. Each new challenge, project, and collaboration will give you the opportunity to deepen your understanding and solidify SharePoint's place as an indispensable part of your work life. Embrace the journey, apply what you've learned, and let SharePoint be the gateway to a more efficient, collaborative, and future-ready work environment.

Printed in Great Britain
by Amazon

58252648R00077